THE WANING
OF THE
OLD SOUTH
CIVILIZATION

THE WANING

OF THE

OLD SOUTH

CIVILIZATION

1860-1880's

CLEMENT EATON

MERCER UNIVERSITY LAMAR
MEMORIAL LECTURES, NO. 10

UNIVERSITY OF GEORGIA PRESS

ATHENS

To

Mary Elizabeth

Spirited Northerner

and to

Allis

Southern Humanist

Contents

Foreword

MERCER UNIVERSITY BRINGS HER LAMAR LECTURE SERIES TO maturity with this tenth volume of published essays on Southern culture, history, and literature. This program of annual lectures was made possible ten years ago by a legacy from a grand Southern lady, the late Mrs. Walter D. Lamar. It was Dorothy Eugenia Blount Lamar's wish that the university-across-the-square provide lectures "of the very highest type of scholarship. . . ." Because of the eminence of the lectures and the high quality of workmanship of the University of Georgia Press which publishes these essays, the series is well established and Mrs. Lamar's dream has become a reality.

Clement Eaton, Professor of History at the University of Kentucky and the author of this volume, measures up in every way to the standard set by his nine predecessors. In interpretation of the intellectual and cultural history of the South no one surpasses him. As the Lamar lecturer for 1966 he presented to sympathetic audiences four lectures under the general theme, "The South in Transition." Through many years of research and writing Professor Eaton has learned the South — learned its people, their virtues and their vices. This enables him to understand the transitional period, 1860-1880.

Some of the previous lectures have dealt with various aspects of the ante-bellum period and others have analysed the New South, but Eaton examines the period in which change slowly began to occur, and in that period he sees a surrender only of what could be legislated out of Southern life—which was very little, and hardly affected customs and attitudes. Indeed, the period was one in which tradition survived. Eaton is not of that breed of historians who casts doubts on the validity of the very term "Southern culture." Instead, he sees a unique people whose culture was not only distinctive before 1860 but whose civilization "waned" most gradually during the twenty-year period of his study.

This volume serves as a bridge connecting past volumes which emphasize the early history of the South and those which study the New South. Others have noted trends beginning after Appomattox, but Professor Eaton has in this volume shown a culture in transition without loss of its identity.

At Professor Eaton's request the Lamar Committee permitted him to develop his thesis beyond his original four lectures by expanding his manuscript to six chapters. The present volume is the result of his skillful and painstaking efforts.

SPENCER B. KING, JR., *Co-Chairman*
The Lamar Lecture Committee

Mercer University
Macon, Georgia

Preface

THIS VOLUME IS THE STORY OF THE EARLY STAGES OF A TRAN-
sition from the Old to the New South. It is based on the concept that, although the Civil War had a traumatic effect on
the Southern spirit, much of the Old South civilization survived the war and lived on into the twentieth century. The
title of the book was suggested by the superb study of the slow
passing of the Middle Ages of western Europe into the Renaissance period by the Dutch scholar, Johan Huizinga, entitled
The Waning of the Middle Ages. Huizinga based his interpretation of the dying spirit of an august civilization in Europe
mainly on a study of the works of art, literature, and thought
of the Middle Ages and the proto-Renaissance. But such
materials as he used in writing his book were only to a slight
degree available to me, for the Old South civilization left
behind it no beautiful Gothic cathedral such as Chartres, no
Rogier von der Weyden or Jan Van Eyck, no brothers Lim-
burg to portray the pageant of its life as they did the life of
the Middle Ages in their illuminations in the Duc de Berry's
book of Hours, no Chastellain, Froissart, or Commines, no
Roman de la Rose, or *Imitation of Christ* by Thomas à Kem-
pis. Indeed, since the Old South was not old but relatively

very young, it had little time to develop either a comparable art, a literature, or an aristocracy in the European sense.

The period of time covered by this study begins with the formation of the Southern Confederacy and ends twenty years later, in the eighteen eighties, when propagandists and reformers, such as Bishop Atticus G. Haygood, Henry Grady, and Sidney Lanier hailed the rise of a "New South." My volume is concerned only incidentally with military or political history during this period—subjects that appear to have been virtually exhausted by recent writers on the history of the Civil War and by the Reconstruction Revisionists. Rather, I seek to explore the currents of social and cultural life that flowed on despite the disaster of a civil conflict. I am fascinated by observing how much of the past survives—it does not die abruptly but wanes gradually and often very slowly, as did the Old South civilization after Appomattox. Indeed, it was not until the Depression decade of the 1930's that one could truthfully write that most of the ante-bellum South had "Gone With the Wind."

The major parts of four of these chapters were given as the Lamar Lectures at Mercer University in the fall of 1966, but since their delivery I have done additional research and have expanded and deepened them. The first two chapters have been added subsequently because I thought that one should portray the Old South civilization—both the folk and the aristocratic culture—as it existed in 1860 before its fate in the next two decades should be told. I wish to thank the Lamar Lecture Committee, the History Department, especially Professor Spencer B. King, Jr., and the President of Mercer University, Dr. Rufus Harris, for giving me the opportunity to write this volume, and for their great kindness to me while I was a guest of the University.

C. E.

History Department
University of Kentucky

ONE

The Southern Folk on the Eve of the Civil War

UNDERLYING THE CULTURE OF A SMALL MINORITY OF ARISTO-
crats in Southern society on the eve of the Civil War was the
encompassing folk culture. Rather than being separate and
contrasted, as in the hierarchial society of the Middle Ages,
the two cultures intermingled—that of the double log cabin
with its "breezeway," or "dog run," consorted with the culture
of the planter's mansion with its white columned piazza and
slave quarters. Many of the aristocrats, especially in the Cotton
Kingdom, were descended from farmers who had hacked from
the wilderness the small farms that later grew into plantations.

The Southern folk consisted mostly of yeoman farmers, but
they included the great majority of the villagers, the overseers,
and the mechanic class; at the bottom of the mass of common
people were the "poor whites" and at the top were some of
the small planters whose culture, habits, and dress were similar
to those of the yeomen. Frederick Law Olmsted, in his *A
Journey in the Back Country* (1860), has described such an

1

individual in his portrait of a prosperous farmer in east Tennessee with whom he spent the night. This farmer-planter owned a number of slaves, extensive fields, considerable herds of cattle and horses, and lived in the best house in the neighborhood, a large, neat, white dwelling. His sons called him "the squire." Yet he went barefooted like the rest of the yeomen and slept in his clothes; his wife smoked a pipe; the family used a common towel. He had only the vaguest ideas of geography and thought that in New York the Irish laborers were enslaved. At a neighboring yeoman's home, the fastidious Northern traveler noticed that there was no window in the log cabin, that the proprietor before retiring at night read the Bible by the light of a candle, spelling out the hard words, and that he prayed with great fervor, assisted by the ejaculatory responses of his wife. Furthermore, the old lady mixed the hoe cakes in the same bowl in which the family washed their faces and hands. Traveling in South Carolina in 1878, another visitor, Sir George Campbell, a Scottish M. P., came across planters who had lived so long on isolated sea island plantations that they talked like the Gullah Negroes and had an outlook no wider than their plantations.

Geographically, Southern folk culture extended beyond the boundaries of the land of "Dixie" into southern Indiana, Illinois, and Ohio. Here was the penumbra of the Greater South—whither the Southern upland stock, including Abraham Lincoln and his family, migrated. Southern folk culture also prevailed in eastern Maryland and southern Missouri. As the Southern upland stock expanded across the Ohio River, they came into cultural conflict with Northern settlers, especially "the cow-milking Yankee Puritans." Their agricultural methods were somewhat different from those of the New England settlers, as were their methods of keeping house, their failure to make cheese, and their speech, education, and religion. Something of their expatriate Southern folk culture and attitudes has been preserved in Edward Eggleston's *The Hoosier Schoolmaster*.

A most perceptive and, on the whole, sympathetic observer of the Southern folk as they were immediately after the Civil War was John William De Forest, a Freedman's Bureau agent stationed in Greenville, South Carolina. In an account of his experiences entitled *A Union Officer in the Reconstruction,* he divided the white population of the uplands that he observed in 1866 into the gentry, whom he called the "Chivalrous Southrons"; the yeomen, or middle class, whom he designated as the "Semi-Chivalrous Southrons"; and the poor whites, whom he described as the "low-down people." De Forest thought that the "low down" people were the descendants of the indentured servants of the colonial period or of the poor human stock cast off from the British Isles. But almost certainly the major cause for their low estate was the adverse environment in which they lived that tended to paralyze ambition and to enervate them by endemic diseases, notably hookworm, malaria, and nutritional diseases. De Forest admitted that the poor whites who entered the Confederate army did their fair share of fighting though many of them were Unionists and evaded the draft or deserted. He observed that their character improved under the discipline of the army, but when they returned to civilian life their native laziness reasserted its old ascendancy, and they relapsed into their former shiftless way of life. He believed that their future improvement would come from the opportunity to do productive work which the rise of the cotton mills would give to them. Sir George Campbell corroborated this prediction in his travel account, *White and Black, the Outcome of a Visit to the United States,* observing that "the white mill workers are a good class of people and very often own their own houses. . . ."

The "Semi-Chivalrous Southrons" were mostly yeoman farmers and the tradesmen and mechanics of the villages, with a sprinkling of small planters, a class whom the Bureau Agent described as honorable worthy people, possessing little education. He cited as a specimen of this middle class a magistrate whom the country people addressed as "the squire"—a

plain poor man dressed in homespun, mild, grave, and honorable, with a strong sense of responsibility. De Forest maintained that the yeoman farmers had absorbed some of the
characteristics of the "Chivalrous Southrons," but he gave few
particulars of the attributes that they had assimilated. William Thomson, a Scottish wool-carder who traveled in the
Southern states in 1840-42 and published a valuable travel
account, wrote, on the other hand, that the common people
of the South, in contrast to Europeans of the same class, were
very polite and considered themselves men of honor, resenting
any indignity shown to them, "even at the expense of their
life or that of those who venture to insult them." It is probable also that their ideas of hospitality and strong interest in
politics were influenced by the practices of the planter gentry.

In order to counteract the stereotype of Southern society
that prevailed in the North on the eve of the Civil War, the
stereotype of a society divided into three classes—the aristocratic planters, a great mass of poor, or "mean," whites, and
the slaves—Daniel R. Hundley in 1860 published a pioneer
sociological study of his native region entitled *Social Relations
in Our Southern States*. Despite his pro-slavery prejudices, his
own stereotyped concept of Northern society, and the inherent
difficulty of a native Southerner obtaining a detached view
of the society in which he had been reared, Hundley was well
qualified for his task of analyzing Southern society. The son
of a middle-class planter and preacher, he grew up on a plantation in northern Alabama, was educated at Bacon College in
Kentucky, the University of Virginia, and Harvard College
where he received a L.L.B. degree in 1853. His brief manuscript diary, which is preserved in the University of North
Carolina Southern Collection, shows that he exhibited many
of the characteristics of the planter class of the lower South.
He was fond of hunting and fishing and of reading books;
he was very religious; he was an ardent secessionist; he served
on a vigilance committee in 1861 that condemned to death

several Negroes for conspiring in an insurrectionary plot; and he was ambitious to be elected captain of a volunteer company that he sought to raise for the defense of the South.

Instead of the two-class white society of the abolitionist stereotype, Hundley divided the Southern whites into four classes: (1) the gentlemen, (2) the middle class, (3) the yeomen, and (4) the "poor whites." The Southern yeoman, he pointed out, constituted a large class of small independent farmers that the abolitionist stereotype wholly neglected. With the exception of the German-descended farmers of western Virginia (and he should have added the German settlers of southern Texas), they were, he declared, from old English stock. Dwelling in large numbers in the Piedmont region and interspersed among the plantations of the low-land region, these farmers were engaged chiefly in cultivating subsistence crops — corn and wheat — and they also raised considerable livestock, particularly hogs. In the cotton country they usually raised a bale or two of cotton and in the tobacco country planted a patch of tobacco in order to earn money to buy a few necessities or luxuries at the village store. They lived in rude log cabins, wore homespun clothing, delighted in hunting and fishing, and were deadly shots with a rifle.

Though many of them were illiterate, probably a third of them, Hundley maintained that in respect to native intelligence they were the peers of the rural population of the North, though not of the city folk, and that they were better versed in politics and in the judgment of good liquor than were their Northern counterparts. Their knowledge of politics was derived, not from reading newspapers, but from listening to orators and from attending barbecues and hearing political discussions at courthouse gatherings and country stores. Henry Benjamin Whipple, a Northerner who traveled in the South earlier than the time of Hundley's book, corroborated the testimony of Hundley, observing that the Georgia "crackers" despite their uncouth language and rough appearance were sharp-witted and intelligent about practical matters; "they have a high estimation of their own qualities," he wrote in his journal, "and look on book 'larnin' as superfluous."

The illiteracy of a large proportion of the Southern people as compared with the Northern people was a distinct weakness of the Confederacy in coping with the enemy. Although the Southern states seem to have had a larger number of college-educated men proportionately to white population than the North, the masses below the Mason and Dixon line were more ignorant than those above. In 1850 the illiteracy ratio among the white population of the Southern states over twenty years of age was 20 to 30 per cent, whereas the ratio in the Middle States was only 3 per cent, and in New England less than 1 per cent. Bell Wiley in his *Life of Johnny Reb* found that in a large sampling of the soldiers of North Carolina regiments 40 per cent of those Tar Heels could not sign their names. This appalling degree of illiteracy was certainly much higher than the average of the Confederate rank and file, but it seems probable that at least one-fourth of those who wore the gray uniforms could neither read nor write.

In the yeoman class Hundley placed the overseers. These men, he declared, had been generally slandered due to the faults and abuse of a minority of them. He regarded them as comparable to the policemen of the North, preserving order on the Southern plantations just as the Northern policemen did in their cities and towns. Although he admitted that there were some brutal, ignorant, and shiftless individuals among them, he asserted that "compared with the police of all other places the world over, and taken en masse, there is not a more respectable and well-behaved patrol than the Southern overseers." A considerable number of overseers were sons of planters; some of them were slave-owners themselves, and some were ambitious to rise into the rank of planters and succeeded in doing so. A profile of the Georgia county of Hancock in 1860, drafted by J. C. Bonner, shows that in this county of

8,137 slaves there were 139 overseers, 20 of whom were sons of planters and 42 of whom lived in the homes of their employers.

Hundley did not use statistics to give clarity and sharpness to his picture of Southern class structure as did Hinton Rowan Helper for propaganda purposes in his *Impending Crisis of the South*. This deficiency was corrected ninety years later by Professor Frank Owsley and his students of Vanderbilt University, who examined the manuscript census returns of 1850 and 1860 to determine the economic position of the various classes of the Old South. By using a sampling process they concluded that the yeoman class formed by far the largest segment of Southern society and that outside of the Carolinas and Virginia 80 per cent of the farmers of the Old South owned the land they cultivated. In North Carolina in 1860 two-thirds of the agricultural units contained less than 100 acres and in Kentucky 76 per cent of the farmers cultivated farms of less than 100 acres.

The characteristics of the Southern folk, as well as the fluidity of Southern society, are illustrated by the career of Alexander H. Stephens, the son of a poor slaveless farmer and an "old field" schoolteacher of middle Georgia. Stephens's mother died shortly after he was born in 1812 and he spent a bleak, cheerless childhood. His frail body was ill-adapted to hard work on his father's farm, for even in manhood he weighed only ninety-seven pounds, stood only five feet seven inches tall, and had a waist measurement of twenty inches. His bloodless face, wrinkled despite its preternaturally boyish appearance, and his dark despairing eyes presented the appearance of a person ready for the grave. He was constantly afflicted with illness, especially with neuralgia, but he lived to be seventy-one years old, not dying until 1883.

With Stephens's political career we are not concerned, except as it reflected characteristics of the Southern yeoman class, but from his letters and from those written to him we can gain some authentic insights into the life of the Southern folk. There are 115 bound volumes of his manuscript papers in the Library of Congress, containing some letters that reveal his inmost thoughts and feelings. Stephens was representative of those numerous sons of the Southern yeoman who were ambitious to rise above their lowly position to political power and places of honor. Money was not his primary goal in life; his intense ambition was to hold political office. In this quest he succeeded admirably, for he served as congressman from 1843 to 1859, was chosen Vice-President of the Confederacy, and after the Civil War was elected to the Senate, though not permitted by the Radicals to take his seat, was once more a congressman from 1873 to 1882, and at the end of his life in 1883 was elected governor of Georgia. Although Stephens sprang from the common people, his political success was not based on folksiness or the arts of the demagogue. In fact, much of his political career was spent in opposing the popular current of the moment, for example, the Mexican War, secession in 1850 and again in 1860, and the major policies of the Confederate government; after the war he cooperated with the Independents.

Nevertheless, he represented some of the distinctive characteristics of the yeomen of Georgia. Stephens had a conservative temperament and outlook on life as did the yeomen as a class. The yeomen, though they delighted in natural pleasures of hunting and fishing, displayed a strong streak of asceticism toward more worldly and sophisticated pleasures, and in this attitude Stephens went to extreme lengths. As a young man, he regarded dancing as a ridiculously undignified activity for human beings. His serious attitude toward life was reflected in his description of the somnolent life of Crawfordville, the village near which his farm was located. On July 20, 1852, he wrote to a political friend that he rode into the village and observed the activities of the citizens. At Gee's grocery, he found some of the villagers sitting on the porch playing or watching two games of drafts that were in progress, the clerk and the village doctor participating in the game while the storekeeper watched through a window. Finding no interest in such idle waste of time, he passed on, but seeing old Billy Lettler sitting on his piazza, he stopped to talk with him; then he went to the cobbler's shop and ordered a pair of shoes made, and later in the day he returned to Gee's store and there saw the same villagers still playing. "What a dull day!" he commented.

Stephens was perhaps most representative of the common people of Georgia in his intense devotion to his farm and home near Crawfordville which he called "Liberty Hall." In 1865 while a prisoner in Fort Warren, Boston, he wrote in his diary: "No mortal ever had stronger attachments for his home than I for mine. That old homestead and that quiet lot, Liberty Hall, in Crawfordville, sterile and desolate as they may seem to others, are bound to me by associations tender as heart strings and strong as hooks of steel. There I wish to live and die." His deep devotion to locality and state was expressed in his politics, both in his career as a national statesman and as Vice-President of the Confederacy, by a staunch upholding of state's rights. His magnum opus, the two-volume *Constitutional View of the War Between the States* (1870), was based firmly on a state's rights interpretation of the United States Constitution.

The Georgia statesman also admirably illustrated the kindly relations that usually existed between the yeoman farmers and their slave helpers. Although the typical yeoman was not a slaveholder, a considerable minority of small farmers owned a few slaves and probably a larger number hired them, as Hinton Rowan Helper maintained in his *Impending Crisis of the South*. When they did own slaves, almost invariably the yeomen and their sons worked with them in the fields. Hundley observed that the relations between the yeoman masters and their slaves were as a rule quite friendly; the slaves of small farmers often called their masters by their first names, drank water from the same dipper and whiskey from the same bottle, and in the turpentine forests often slept in the same tent as their master.

Stephens, who started out as a poor boy, eventually became a considerable slaveowner. From the profits of his law practice, by 1850, he had been able to acquire 5,000 acres of land, scattered in different parts of the state, and thirteen slaves. Ten years later he had added further acres and more slaves to his estate so that he held $53,000 worth of property and 32 slaves. In the Stephens Papers in the Library of Congress there is a letter from Alexander to his half-brother Linton, dated November 29, 1853, which eloquently reveals his attitude toward his slaves. Linton was eleven years younger than his famous brother, a large handsome man to whom the diminutive Stephens was passionately devoted. It was Stephens who provided the money to educate Linton at the University of Virginia and at Harvard Law School. He wrote constantly to Linton and in these letters he bared his melancholy mind and soul. On November 29, 1853, when he was forced to stop at Augusta on his way to Washington by a severe headache, the recurrence of which often incapacitated him, he wrote to Linton about the will that he had just made. He was especially concerned for the fate of his slaves after his death, and to his brother whom he wished to inherit his slaves he wrote: "If you should not be in life [at the time of my death] to take charge of my negroes and be to them a master to whom they could and would look with even affection for protection, I would rather send them to Liberia than they should be scrambled over by John and Green [Stephens's other relatives], and scattered to the four quarters of the globe—or that they should, as they might, fall into strange and to them unknown hands during the minority of your children. . . ." In the same letter he commented on one of his slaves, Harry, who acted as his valet, at times accompanying him to Washington, "I almost cried yesterday when Harry left me."

In a slender volume among the Stephens Papers marked "Servant's Letters, 1867-1883" are some letters to Stephens from his former slaves which show the affectionate feelings that they continued to hold toward their former master. These letters are remarkably literate for Negroes brought up in slavery. Dora, apparently his cook and housekeeper at "Liberty Hall," wrote in 1873 a most affectionate letter to "Master Elex" in Washington, telling him that she felt sad that he was so far from home and that she could not see his frail figure sitting, as formerly, in his room with his hat on, but she informed him that she was taking good care of his dog. In 1874 she wrote that she had read the "speach that you sent me," and that "Uncle Josh says he thinks of what good drams you used to give him and hopes that you will get back safe [to Liberty Hall] to give him more. I am trying to be a good girl and hope I will hold out. . . ." Harry wrote to Stephens in the same year from Crawfordville, telling him of his success in raising cotton and the money he had made from ginning white people's cotton and how he missed Stephens's "good talks" and advice that had helped to keep him solvent while so many white farmers were in economic distress. On December 3, 1874, after Harry had returned to Georgia from Washington, he wrote to Stephens that he had hated to leave him, especially "when you shake my hand and told me if we never meet again you hope to meet in heaven." Other letters from former slaves indicate that Stephens was paying for the education of some of their children. Yet there was a deep irony in Stephens's attitude toward slaves, for he is famous for the statement in his inaugural address as Vice-President of the Confederacy that the newly created republic was based on the cornerstone of slavery.

By the 1850's Stephens had risen into the ranks of the small planters, and among his closest friends were aristocratic large planters such as Robert Toombs and Howell Cobb. His career was a demonstration that the gradations in rank between the yeomen and the small planters, and between the latter and the middle-size planters were not strongly marked in Southern society; one class merged into the other. In addition to the strong imprint of the frontier and the influence of Lockian philosophy, the existence of Negro slavery contributed greatly to a sense of equality among all whites in the South, or, as Calhoun expressed it, a Greek type of democracy.

Hundley in his analysis of Southern society of the ante-bellum period distinguished a middle class between the yeoman and the gentry. In this class he placed the more prosperous farmers and the small planters, who formed the bulk of this class, to which he added the "half-fledged" country lawyers, doctors, parsons, and teachers of "old field" schools. Apparently he regarded the more sophisticated and richer lawyers and merchants of the large towns and cities as belonging to the upper class of Southern society. He traced the origin of the members of the middle class to the franklins and thanes of England with a little intermixture of Norman blood. He observed that some of the most notable political leaders of the South, such as Jefferson, Patrick Henry, and Calhoun, had come from this class. Accordingly he doubtless would have placed Stephens also in this class and perhaps noted that his paternal ancestor who had migrated to America in 1746 was a soldier who had fought in the battle of Culloden Moor for Prince Charles.

The members of the middle class, Hundley noted, were usually slaveholders who owned from five to fifty slaves. The small planters generally managed their slaves without employing an overseer. If they did hire an overseer, the latter ate at the table with the small planter's family and could hardly be distinguished from him, so similar in dress, speech, and manners were the two. In the majority of cases, Hundley asserted that the small planters were kind to their slaves, especially to the inherited or "family slaves," called them "Uncle" and "Auntie," and consulted the old, experienced slaves, who advised them, for example, as to when the moon was right for planting, or other folk superstitions in reference to cultivating crops. The small planters included their slaves in the family circle for the morning and evening reading of the Bible and the kneeling at prayer. Like the yeomen, they were usually devout and belonged to the Baptist or Methodist denomination, while the gentry chose the Episcopalian way to Heaven. Some of the more devout and emotional among them attended camp meetings in the summer with the yeomen, but Hundley observed in 1860 that camp meetings had in recent years been falling into disrepute in the South. Like the yeomen, too, they were very independent and did not truckle to persons of superior wealth or position. Unlike the New Englanders of their class, they would not tolerate "the isms" that Hundley said "disgraced" the free states. The small planters, he declared, looked much like the gentry, without having the polish or "airy and graceful carriage" of the upper class.

It is surprising to find that this perceptive observer of Southern society included in the middle class the mechanics, skilled laborers, and "a few manufacturers," for they would seem to belong to the yeoman class. It was true, Hundley admitted, they did not have the same social position as the high-bred Southern gentleman, but such was the case in every society. Nevertheless, the mechanic class was, he wrote, as much respected in the South as anywhere in the world. Indeed, the Southern mechanics, he pointed out, were much better off than the Northern mechanics, because there was less competition for work among them (he did not mention that they were often in competition with slaves and free Negro mechanics), they received better wages, and could work out-of-doors the year round.

A valuable but relatively unexplored source for studying the mores of the Southern folk is to be found in the local color writings of the Southern humorists. The most important of these writers after the Civil War was Richard Malcolm

Johnston. In his short stories and sketches he realistically, yet with a touch of nostalgia, portrayed the life of the country people of the ante-bellum Georgia of his youth. Colonel Johnston had the experience, the sympathetic imagination, and the observant eye to record faithfully the characteristics of the common people of his native section. The son of a planter and unsalaried Baptist preacher, Johnston was born on a plantation near Powelton, Georgia, in 1822. Small farmers, "the crackers," were often neighbors of the planters, and Richard moved freely with their children as well as with the little Negroes on the plantation. From these childhood contacts he learned the vernacular of the common people, "the cracker dialects," which he faithfully recorded in his short stories. In explaining the reason why he never "slipped up" in the use of the dialect in his writings, he said that it came naturally to him as a result of his early associations. Johnston was educated in an "old field" school taught by a Vermont Yankee and in the manual labor institute that became Mercer University. His intercourse with the common people, however, was maintained by his constant association with them during his career as a young lawyer in the courts of northern and middle Georgia.

In traveling the circuit as a lawyer Colonel Johnston had displayed a talent for telling amusing stories. Moreover, he had an example of vivid delineation of folkways and antics of the "crackers" and yeomen in the writings of ante-bellum Georgia humorists, especially Augustus Baldwin Longstreet and William Tappan Thompson. In 1857 he published his first sketch, "A Georgia School in the Old Times" in William T. Porter's *Spirit of the Times*. After Johnston moved to Baltimore in 1867, Sidney Lanier helped him to make his stories of rural Georgia more artistic by his frank criticism, praising him highly for "his reproduction of the modes of thought and of speech among the rural Georgians," but also pointing out a weakness, namely that his stories did not move fast enough "to suit the impatience of the modern magazine man."

Colonel Johnston's first book of importance was his *Dukesborough Tales,* published in 1871 in Baltimore, Maryland, under the *nom de plume* of "Philemon Perch," and for which he received no money. The stories in it are descriptive of the village life of Powelton and its surroundings. "The Goosepond School" and "How Mr. Bill Williams Took the Responsibility" are stories that came from his experience of attending an "old field" school in ante-bellum Georgia, and they are vivid social documents, as much so as his publication, while he held a job under the U. S. Commissioner of Education, of a report entitled "Early Educational Life in Middle Georgia," (*Report,* 1894-1895, II, 1699-1733). Johnston regarded his literary career as starting in 1879 when *Scribner's Monthly* published in its June issue, "Mr. Neelus Peeler's Conditions," for which he received his first check for a literary production. Thereafter he was able to publish other Southern stories in northern magazines. The previous year he had in cooperation with William Hand Browne published a biography of Alexander H. Stephens, who was still living and with whom he had had many conversations. In 1888 he published *Mr. Absalom Billingslea and Other Georgia Folk;* in 1891, *The Primes and Their Neighbors;* and in 1898, the year of his death, *Old Times in Middle Georgia.* These were all collections of stories, but he also published three novels about Southern life: *Old Mark Langston* (1883), *Widow Guthrie* (1893), and *Pearce Amerson's Will* (1898).

Colonel Johnston, like the Kentuckian James Lane Allen, wrote in the traditional genteel style. Since that style went out of fashion in the early twentieth century his work is largely forgotten. A gentleman of the old school, his personality entered very much into the character of his stories of ante-bellum Georgia. The 1880 edition of his *Dukesborough Tales* contains his portrait in the frontispiece, and shows a fine, aristocratic face, adorned with a large flowing white mustache and an amiable expression. Grace King who met him in his old age described him as "a typical Southerner in voice and manner ... erect of figure, with white hair and mustache, a genial, witty, unaffected talker, full of good stories, interesting to everybody." He was tall, slender, and courtly.

Colonel Johnston's descriptions of rural Georgia before and after the war emphasized the lack of consciousness of class divisions and distinctions among the Georgians. Indeed, their democratic way of life seems to have been characteristic of the South as a whole with the exception of coastal Virginia, South Carolina, and a few enclaves such as Natchez. Johnston's sketches certainly tend to modify the romantic stereotype of the Old South which exalts the planter as an aristocratic figure. In his introduction to *Mr. Absalom Billingslea and Other Georgia Folk* he wrote, "In this region, very fertile and almost universally salubrious, perhaps there was as little of social distinctions among its inhabitants as among those of any other in the South. The men of culture and those of wealth, as a general thing, were neighbors of the uncultured, and those with moderate or small property around them, and all were friends of one another. . . ."

He maintained also that many well-educated Georgians, including some of the most eminent lawyers, used the Georgia dialect and country expressions in preference to the more correct formal English, but that this practice of using colloquialisms was less prevalent among the women than the men, and he warned his readers against regarding the colloquial speech as an index of culture.

The Southern humorists, such as Colonel Johnston and his predecessors, Longstreet, Thompson, Hooper, and Harris, vividly described the appearance of the Southern folk. The men did not shave or "dress up" except on Sunday or special occasions. When one of Colonel Johnston's characters, Absalom Billingslea, bought a tall beaver fur hat and a broadcloth frock coat, dressed his long hair with bear grease, and anointed himself with cinnamon perfume, in order to court the widow Ashley, he astonished the inhabitants of "Dukesborough" by wearing such finery on a week-day—"a thing that the oldest inhabitant had never known of having been done except by a marrying man specifically and avowedly intent upon immediate pressing courtship." The ordinary attire of the Southern countrymen of this period as they rode to market was described by Olmsted in 1853 as consisting of "long-skirted homespun coats, slouch hats, and heavy boots outside of their trousers."

The dress of the female portion of the country people and villagers was also decidedly lacking in style, although when they dressed in calico to receive company or go to church they put on stays or corsets. The young girls wore pantalettes beneath their dresses, and it was a sign of adolescence when they, according to the rural Georgia expression, "drapped their pantalettes," or no longer wore them, and lengthened their dresses. Whenever the women did not go barefoot, as they usually did, they wore thick gray stockings, but in this Victorian age to mention stockings before a gentleman was regarded as immodest. When "Major Jones" the Georgia country bumpkin of Thompson's stories, visited the home of Mary Stallings to "pop the question," she and her sisters blushed deeply at the mention of stockings by the old lady Stallings and rebuked their mother. The aristocratic city ladies wore crinoline or hoop skirts. Kate Stone of Brockenburn Plantation recorded in her diary while she was a refugee in Texas during the war that she saw cracker girls dressed in coal scuttle bonnets and huge hoop skirts beneath which protruded their bare feet.

In his earthy stories of Middle Georgia, Colonel Johnston recorded some of the distinctive social attitudes of the rural folk, many of which survived long after the Civil War. A number of his sketches described the schools of the old time, such as "The Goosepond School Story," which tells of the rural belief that a teacher had to whip his students often in order to instruct them properly, and of the custom of studying aloud in the school room. Some of his stories revolve around the convention that prescribed the necessity of a suitor for a girl's hand to obtain the permission of her father in order to marry her (a custom that also prevailed in the North). He described the role of the country store as a focus of masculine social life; the petty quarrels that often arose between women of adjoining farms because of the encroachment of their flocks of geese on each other's property; rural superstitions, such as using the divining rod to locate well sites, and planting at the right time of the moon; the high value that Southern farmers placed on having good springs on their property; and the neighborly custom, necessitated by semi-frontier conditions, of nursing each other during severe sickness (an illustration narrated in "The Durance of Mr. Dickerson Prime"). He sketched the lights and shadows of rural life produced by the impact of the institution of slavery, the loyalty of some slaves to their masters (in the stories, "Moll and Virgil," and "Travis and Major Wilby"), the tragedies brought about by the bankruptcy of extravagant planters, or by the planters' habit of endorsing the notes of friends and as a result being forced to sell some of their trusted slaves for whom they had a real affection. He gave an insight into some of the crude vestiges of the frontier that still lingered over the Southern life on the eve of the Civil War, such as his story of the preacher ("Reverend Rainsford Gunn and the Arab Chief") who subdued a rowdy gang of young fellows who tried to break up church services.

One of the most interesting aspects of Southern folk culture was the remedies used for the cure and prevention of disease. When Doctor Francis P. Porcher, a professor at the Medical College of Charleston, published during the Civil War a six hundred page book entitled *Resources of the Southern Fields and Forests,* describing the native herbs, roots, and trees which were valuable for making drugs, medicines, and substitutes, he relied partly on folk empirics for his prescriptions. Some of the folk remedies were not only naive but absurd, such as the custom that Mrs. Rebecca Felton tells about in her *Country Life in Georgia in the Days of My Youth* of girls wearing little bags of stinking assafoetida suspended on a cord around their necks to prevent itch.

A good picture of Southern folk medicine is given in "Martin Marshall's Book" which Weymouth T. Jordan has edited under the title *Herbs, Hoecakes, and Husbandry*. In the course of a long life Martin Marshall, a South Carolina yeoman who moved in 1815 to Alabama where he farmed and practiced the trades of weaver and blacksmith, collected the lore of folk medicine and recorded it in a manuscript of 450 pages, entitled "Martin Marshall's Book." In this curious work he wrote down the homely cures for various diseases that were used by the Southern folk. These remedies were purely empiric, the result of the observation of trying many different herbs, vegetables, roots, barks, and flowers of the field and forests. One wonders how many bald men were able to grow hair on their heads as a result of his remedy for baldness, namely, to rub the bald part of the skull morning and evening with onions until it became red, and afterwards rub it with honey. Was there any mysterious curative power in his remedy for rheumatism, namely an ointment made from boiling the blooms of the Jimson weed with tobacco, red pepper, and lard; or in treating whooping cough with wild ginger; or in his cure for the bite of a poisonous snake by making a powder made from a buzzard's maw combined with a plaster of turpentine and drinking a solution of the juice of the cockle burr and strong tobacco? His cure for the yaws was to purge with jalap and calomel; and for the King's evil, the application of an ointment made of malt and the inner bark of the white oak tree. In order to drive warts away he advised rubbing them with a snail that had shed its shell. The cure for the disease of gleet was to be effected by drinking a concoction made from the weed called stinking orrace; for the thrush, by gargling rose water mixed with honey; and for the shingles, by applying an ointment of elder bark, gunpowder, and cream. To combat an attack of venereal disease he prescribed heroic doses of mercury, corrosive sublimate, laudanum, calomel, opium, sassafras root tea, black haw root, sumac root, and slippery elm tea. Surely such a wide range of remedies fired at random would hit a target, and either cure or kill the patient. As for Martin Marshall, he lived to be eighty-three years old.

The characteristics and mores of the Southern folk were mirrored in some of their peculiar personal habits and crude amusements. Dipping snuff and smoking a corncob pipe by females seem to have been confined largely to women of the lower class, but chewing tobacco was practiced widely by aristocrats and common men. The practice of tobacco chewing continued long after the Civil War; Sir George Campbell discovered when he was in Atlanta in 1878 that it took real nerve to cross the lobby of the principal hotel, the Kimball House, because of the imminent danger of being hit by a stream of tobacco juice. The amusements of the common people differed in some respects from those of the gentry, in that they retained the frontier sports of shooting for the prize of a beef or a turkey, "gander pulling," corn huskings, log rolling and house raisings, pitching horse shoes in front of stores or on the court house grounds, quilting parties, singing school in the rural churches, practical joking and telling tall stories, bee hunting, or tracing the flight of wild bees to their hives for honey.

The Southern folk were also passionately fond of cock fighting, which was not banned in the Southern states until after the Civil War. Even when the laws later forbad this cruel sport, it continued surreptitiously—as late as the 1960's cock fights were held in Kentucky. The German traveler, Ernst von Hesse-Wartegg, in his *Nord Amerika* (1879) gives a vivid account (in German) of witnessing *Ein Hahnenkampf* in New Orleans. It was an interstate fight between champion cocks of Kentucky and of Georgia. There were no women spectators, only a motley crowd of men, and dense tobacco smoke and the strong smell of alcohol filled the atmosphere. The fighting cocks, the Kentucky one, red in color, the Georgian, black, were armed with steel spurs, three inches long, and finely honed, which were strapped to their legs. There were "backers," or handlers of the birds, and referees, much like the officials at prize fights. The Kentucky cock mutilated his opponent and nearly killed him in the course of the savage fight. The spectators bet excitedly on the outcome of the fight, and the New Orleans newspapers reported it in detail, expressing, Hesse-Wartegg commented, no word of pity or condemnation.

In comparison with their Northern counterparts the Southern folk were remarkably pugnacious. Although they did not practice dueling as did the aristocrats, the common people frequently engaged in fist fights and assaults with knives, hoes, scythes, and axes. Augustus Baldwin Longstreet in *Georgia Scenes* and Colonel Johnston in his story "The Humors of Jacky Bundle" have described the common man's delight in ante-bellum Georgia in promoting and witnessing fights between champions of different villages or from different parts of the same county. A modern study of crime in South Carolina during the ante-bellum period, Jack Williams's *Vogues in Villainy,* which is based on an examination of approximately ten thousand indictments, documents the penchant for violence in the common people of the ante-bellum South. His study reveals that 60 per cent of the indictments were for assault and battery, while only 4 per cent were for murder, and 2 per cent for bastardy. Stemming from this pugnacity of the common people was the development of a striking martial spirit in the Old South, which was nourished by the militia musters and exhibited by the greater amount of volunteering from the South in wartime than from the rest of the country.

Despite their pugnacity and outbursts of violence, the Southern folk were on the whole a deeply religious people. Almost to a man they were fundamentalists in belief whether they belonged to a church or not. In some of his stories of ante-bellum Georgia such as "Suicidal Tendencies of Ephrodtus Twilley," "Our Witch," and "The Experiment of Miss Sally Cash," Colonel Johnston has sketched some of the religious mores of the Southern folk on the eve of the Civil War. He has described their strong puritanical streak — his own father at the age of thirty-five gave up dancing, card-playing, fox hunting, and mint juleps — to be ordained a Baptist preacher. Johnston portrayed the influential role of deacons in advising the flocks and in keeping them on the straight and narrow path. Not all the common people of the South were devout but, with the exception of the "poor whites," a large proportion of them were religious. Of this type no better illustration could be found than a yeoman farmer of Mississippi, Ferdinand Steel, whose manuscript diary for the years 1838-46 has been preserved. Steel lived a life of laborious toil and deprivation but he sustained himself by the comforts of a religion that was oriented to the life beyond the grave. His was a highly emotional, non-rational religion, a social cement for lonely country people, who met at camp meetings and "protracted meetings" to sing hymns, shout on occasions, weep, hear fervid sermons, and reclaim sinners from worldly pleasures. It was a faith rooted in medieval beliefs and warped often by denominational quarrels. Yet it was full of humility and trust in the mysterious ways of Providence and exerted a great moral influence.

The isolation of the Southern folk, the traditions brought by their forefathers from Europe, the influence of the frontier, a warm climate, and the presence of the Negroes in large numbers — all contributed to the development of the peculiar characteristics of Southern folk culture. The mountain whites, especially, preserved old traditions, such as ballads and melancholy songs and tunes brought from the British Isles, folklore, and archaic speech of the seventeenth and eighteenth centuries, and handicraft arts, notably the making of beautiful quilts. Besides the superstitions of the mountain people, the yeomen of the Piedmont and coastal plain absorbed some of the Negro superstitions — as did the planters' children. The provincialism and large degree of illiteracy of the Southern folk were poignantly described by Phoebe Pember, a Jewish widow from Charleston, who served as a matron in the great Chimborazo Military Hospital at Richmond during the Civil War. She had an unusual opportunity to observe the Southern folk as they faced desperate sickness and death in a military hospital, a story which she has told in *A Southern Woman's Story.* Every day she encountered the Southern folk — not only the dying and convalescent soldiers, but even more revealing, the relatives who visited them. They came from the villages, the mountains, and remote farms to see their wounded and dying sons, lovers, and husbands. Many of these visitors were ignorant, snuff-dipping women, poorly clad, crude in speech and awkward in manner, but their devotion to their kin and their religious faith were touching. Phoebe Pember reflected that the provincialism and ignorance they displayed revealed the tremendous neglect of the Southern states in educating the masses.

The picture of the mores and characteristics of the common people of the Old South is only a part of the full pageant of Southern civilization as it existed on the eve of the Civil War. Colonel Johnston in describing the idiosyncrasies and virtues of the common folk of "Dukesborough" realized this fact, and to balance the picture he planned to write stories about the upper class of the village and surrounding country. But he was never able to complete his portrait of Southern life before it began to change in the latter part of the nineteenth century. A member of the *Century Magazine* staff, Mrs. Sophia Bledsoe Herrick, who published an article about Colonel Johnston in that magazine in 1888 while he was still living, wrote that he had said the upper class of his native village "was equal in refinement and culture to any society he has ever known, and somewhat peculiar." It is this upper class of Southern society, the aristocratic planter group, that forms the theme of the following chapter—especially their culture as it different from the common folk, and the question of whether the aristocrats really controlled Southern society in 1860-61.

TWO

Characteristics of the
Planter Aristocracy in 1860

JUST AS THE SECRET DIARY OF WILLIAM BYRD II OF WESTOVER
revealed that the life of the colonial aristocrats of Virginia only
faintly resembled the stately image of the romantic stereotype,
so the diaries of Southern planters of the ante-bellum period
also portray a way of life that does not comport with the
glamorous legend of the Old South. The most serious error in
this legend that the historical revisionists, such as John Spencer
Bassett, U. B. Phillips, Lewis C. Gray, and Frank L. Owsley,
have corrected is the vast exaggeration of the numerical importance of the planters in the structure of Southern society
of the ante-bellum period. An important index of how many
large planters there were in the South of 1860 was the number
who owned enough slaves to justify the employment of an
overseer. A recent scholarly study of the Southern overseer by
William K. Scarborough, entitled *The Overseer; Plantation
Management in the Old South,* shows that in 1860 there were
only approximately 3,800 overseers in the United States. Since

there were at the same time 46,274 persons in a white population of nearly eight million in the Southern states listed by the Census Bureau as planters (as distinguished from farmers) who owned as many as twenty slaves, it is evident that only a small minority of the "planters" employed overseers. The elite plantation group — the Southern aristocracy in general— was considerably larger, of course, than 3,800, for to this number must be added some planters like Bennet Barrow of West Feliciana Parish in Louisiana, who, disgusted with overseers, supervised his plantation with its two hundred slaves himself, using a slave foreman as his assistant.

The geographical distribution in 1860 of "the proud race of country-gentlemen" who owned in excess of one hundred slaves was as follows: Louisiana, 547, South Carolina, 449, Alabama, 346, Mississippi 316, Georgia 212, North Carolina, 133, and Virginia, 114. Most of them lived in the rich soil areas of the South with easy access by water transportation to markets for their staple crops. A recent study of the original manuscript returns of the federal census of 1860 of Louisiana by Joseph K. Menn, entitled *The Large Slaveholders of Louisiana — 1860,* gives a statistical profile of the economically privileged group in one Southern state. It shows that the largest slaveholder and sugar producer in Louisiana was John Burnside, a Scottish immigrant to New Orleans, who made a fortune in commerce, and then bought plantations and slaves, becoming the owner of 940 slaves and total real and personal property valued at $2,600,000. The list of the fifteen largest slaveholders in Louisiana on the eve of the Civil War seems to contain the name of only one Creole owner. Only two of the dozen largest sugar planters, Thomas O. Moore, governor of the state at the time of secession, and Duncan F. Kenner, whom Jefferson Davis sent on a last desperate mission to Europe, were politically active. They were too busy managing their great estates and making money to engage in the fickle game of politics.

Frederick Jackson Turner pointed out that the American frontier bred certain unique qualities in its inhabitants; even more so, the Southern plantation and the autocratic control over Negro slaves left a strong imprint upon the personality of the Southern aristocracy. Daniel R. Hundley, himself a member of an Alabama planter family, has recorded in his *Social Relations in Our Southern States* some observations and generalizations about this unique class in American society —the Southern country gentlemen—that on the whole seem valid. He did not regard the Southern gentleman as the conventional type, such as one would see in the North or on the continent, one who had read Lord Chesterfield, but as "peculiarly the outgrowth of the institutions of the South." Yet even in the Southern states, he admitted, gentlemen were "not quite so plentiful as blackberries in summer time." In portraying the Southern gentleman Hundley began with his pedigree, noting that "family pride prevails to a greater extent in the South than in the North." Here he followed the legend that had already developed, of asserting a descent from English Cavaliers, though he admitted that because of intermarriage between sons and daughters of the gentry and of the middle class (such was the case of Jefferson, for example) there were scattered through the Southern states many gentlemen "whose ancestry was only in part of Cavalier stock." The Southern gentleman, according to this pioneer Southern sociologist, was usually tall, about six feet in height, having a physique derived partly from his ancestry, but also from his healthy out-of-doors life (he might have mentioned also the fact that his nutrition was better than that of the lower class). He scorned the Northern idea that these gentlemen farmers were lazy and lived a soft life. No longer true in 1860, he wrote, was the Sir Roger de Coverley image of the Southern gentleman, for the typical planter on the eve of the Civil War lived "a plain, unostentatious mode of life"; "the Southern gentleman of to-day," he declared, "is less an idler and dreamer than he was in the old

days, is more practical, and although not so great a lover of
the almighty dollar as his Northern kinsman, still is far from
being as great a spendthrift as his fathers were before him."

As to his education, the Southern gentleman, he observed,
spent much of his time close to nature, hunting, fishing, swim-
ming, and riding horses. In his boyhood he was sent to the
nearest "old field school" or academy, riding to school accompanied by a Negro attendant, who shared his lunch at recess.
"Cuffee," mounted on a mule, usually also accompanied him
on fox hunts, a sport which had declined in popularity from
earlier days, especially in the lower South where the red fox
was not so plentiful and the sport had been succeeded by deer
hunting. In all these sports the Negro was a frequent com-
panion of the white man, and as a result they developed cordial relations with each other. The out-of-doors life of the
Southerners, which in a warmer climate could be pursued
through the year, tended to make them less nervous than the
town and city man of the North, as well as less subject to
"fanaticism." When the young Southern aristocrat reached
college age his preferred school was the University of Virginia.
While Hundley himself was attending this institution, there
were enrolled about five hundred students, of whom he estimated about a hundred were dissipated; but of this group, not
more than a dozen were the sons of gentlemen, the rest being
sons of "new-rich swells," or "cotton snobs," and the so-called
"State students," poor boys whose tuition was paid by the
state. The true Southern gentleman was restrained by family
pride from engaging in disgraceful dissipation.

As the outstanding characteristics of the Southern aristocrat,
Hundley claimed for him a natural dignity of manner that he
attributed to the habitual use of authority and to great self
respect, a remarkably easy and natural manner of poise, never
being loud in speech, and the exercise of a gracious hospitality.
Though he admitted that some of the Southern aristocrats
possessed prejudices of caste, he maintained they were no more

class conscious than gentlemen the world over. Family ties in the South, Hundley thought, among both the aristocrats and the plain people were much stronger than in the North and parental discipline was more rigid. Southern girls especially were taught modesty, respect for parents, and abhorrence of the conduct of the "strong-minded" women of the North who advocated women's rights. The Southern gentleman was more interested in and better versed in politics than his Northern counterpart, his views generally being conservative. Hundley claimed that the Southern gentleman was not at all influenced by the world-wide denunciation of slavery—an institution, according to him, of patriarchal benevolence and one sanctioned by the Bible. Much criticism had been made of the practice of dueling in the South but Hundley did not consider it very prevalent among the Southern aristocracy, and undoubtedly it has been exaggerated in romantic accounts of the South. Most Southerners, indeed, never engaged in a duel in their lives.

Some Northern travelers in the South sought to analyze and describe the peculiar characteristics of the Southern gentry that distinguished it from the upper class of the North. Among these observers and commentators was Henry Benjamin Whipple, a very intelligent young Northerner who traveled during 1842-43 in the Southern states for his health (later in life he was to become the Episcopal Bishop of Minnesota). "The southerner himself is different from the northerner in many striking particulars," Whipple wrote in his diary on December 12, 1843. "He is more chivalrous, that is to say, he has more of the old English feeling common in the days of the feudal system & crusades. He is liberal in his feelings, high minded, a warm & generous friend but a malignant and bitter enemy. He forms his attachments easier and does not retain them as long as men of a less ardent disposition. He is generous to a fault with his property (goes surety for friends and often loses his property as a result), is fond of gaiety and pleasure &

generally dislikes the routine of business. His habits are those of genteel idleness or of the man of leisure. Nothing is a too expensive for the gratification of appetite or feeling, which his purse will permit him to buy. There are some gentlemen however that I have met who differ in very many particulars from the above description and whose habits of life are those of a prudent & careful business man. But these I may say are the exceptions."

Another Northerner who came later and stayed longer in the South than Whipple and who was especially perceptive was John William De Forest. He thought that the "Chivalrous Southrons" whom he observed in South Carolina shortly after the Civil War, were a different breed of people than were the Northerners, as unlike in characteristics as were the Spartans and the Athenians or the Poles and the Germans. "They are more simple than we," he wrote, "more provincial, more antique, more picturesque; they have fewer of the virtues of modern society, and more of the primitive, the natural virtues; they care less for wealth, and learning and other delicacies of an urban civilization; they care more for individual character and reputation of honor." He observed that students in Southern colleges and universities practiced a high code of honor in regard to examinations that would be the envy of the faculties of Harvard and Yale.

He was greatly impressed by the cult of virility among all classes of Southern society, which he described as "the central trait of the Chivalrous Southron." The Southerner, he declared, admired excessively the individual who was manly and natural in personality, brave, masculine, good with the rifle and in handling a fractious horse, willing to fight for his honor or his homeland. He had no use for "a sissy" and this attitude extended to condemning boys or men who engaged in such feminine arts as playing the piano (Maunsel White, the prominent New Orleans merchant and planter, for example, peremptorily refused his son's request to be allowed to take piano lessons, or to waste his time "drumming" on the piano, and Bishop Atticus G. Haygood of Georgia was deeply chagrinned that his son wished to study piano music in Boston). De Forest wrote, doubtless with some exaggeration: "Self-respect, as the Southerners understood it, has always demanded much fighting." With sly amusement, he described the reactions of a "high-toned" Southerner walking on Broadway in New York, glaring at and swearing at those in the crowd that jostled him without apologizing.

With all of his virtues and charms, the "high-toned" Southern gentlemen had pronounced defects and limitations. The institution of slavery tended to make many of the planters autocratic and opinionated, for they ruled over their plantations like little kings and were not accustomed to having their wills crossed or opinions contradicted. They did not keep up their property as did the English squires and there was in many plantation homes an air of shiftlessness and untidiness owing to lazy and careless servants. Their young sons were often tempted into ways of immorality by contact with the Negro servants and both boys and girls were rendered lazy by having slave valets and maids assigned to them. Slavery, indeed, tended to denigrate menial and even manual labor. While both master and mistress were often industrious, their children had nothing to do but amuse themselves by hunting, fishing, riding horses, visiting, and drinking.

Although the majority of owners of large plantations were democratic in manners, a minority fitted the description of the large planters of Talbot County in eastern Maryland given by Dr. Samuel A. Harrison, a well-educated native of the Eastern Shore, a slave-owner, but a strong Unionist and advocate of emancipation, in his journal, April 20, 1863: "The wealthy are generally refined in their manners, very proud in their bearings, and very exclusive in their social intercourse. They have the ordinary intelligence of our people at large, neither more nor less well informed, but as a body, are

probably more polite and accomplished in their manners."
The proud, exclusive type of Southern aristocrat was typified
by Colonel Edward Lloyd of Wye House, the largest slaveholder in Maryland, whose sumptuous style of living and autocratic personality Frederick Douglass witnessed as a slave on
the plantation and described so vividly in his autobiography.

A rich source for studying the psychology and the way of
life of a Virginia planter on the eve of the Civil War is found
in the extensive diary of Doctor Richard C. Eppes (manuscript in the Alderman Library of the University of Virginia).
His diary is particularly revealing concerning the influence
of slavery upon the planter. Eppes was graduated from the
University of Virginia in 1842 at the age of eighteen years.
He studied medicine at the University, and among his papers
preserved in the Alderman Library are his carefully-written
notebooks, containing his notes on materia medica, chemistry,
and political economy. After graduation he had inherited the
ancestral plantations and thereafter he devoted himself to agriculture, so much so that in 1859 he wrote in his diary of his
refusal to take a medical case because he was out of practice
in the medical art and was unprepared to doctor people
because of lack of study.

By 1851 Eppes was the master of sixty slaves and the owner
of two plantations in coastal Virginia, the Bermuda Hundreds
Plantation on the Appomattox River, containing 787 acres,
and the Island Plantation of 677 acres; at the time when
Federal troops invaded the state, his slave holdings had increased to 127 slaves and he owned three plantations. Eppes
must have been a very successful manager of slaves, although
the fact that during the Civil War when they had a chance
to escape all but thirteen left him might raise some questions
concerning his paternalism. Nevertheless, he seems to have
been a considerate but firm master who practiced a system
of rewards so that his slaves could earn small sums of money.
In September 1852 he promised rewards of $1 a week to the

best ploughman, and to the ploughman who kept his team in the best condition and least galled, a reward of 50¢. On December 26, 1859, he recorded in his diary that he paid twenty-three field hands at the Island Plantation $42.25 and two days later he paid Madison, the butler, $10; the cook, $5; the assistant cook, $1, of which 50¢ was for making good coffee; the gardener, $2, although he noted that he deserved nothing; Patty, $1, which he wrote was 50¢ too much; Toby, $5, for good ploughing; Stewart, the foreman, $5; and the overseer, George Conway, $250. When wild hogs destroyed some of his corn crop he offered the Negroes $1.50 for each predator they killed.

On the other hand, he maintained strict discipline by whipping the slaves for offences against what he called "the laws of the plantation." On April 2, 1852, he whipped William for leaving the plantation without a pass; on Sunday, April 13, he recorded that he planned to whip one of his slaves for negligence, but after attending church he decided to let him off and commented in his diary that he was becoming more lenient than formerly. "Why," he asked himself, and he philosophized that "the spirit of God is at work in my bosom." But the spirit of God seems to have left him on subsequent occasions; on April 16, he whipped George "for not bringing over milk for my coffee, being compelled to take it without"; on Sunday, July 21, 1852, he flogged Dick for stealing sugar and telling a lie and he corrected Tom for galloping one of his carriage horses; on August 18, 1859, he ordered a whipping for Giles for letting cows get into a cornfield; on September 2, he wrote in his diary, "Today should truly be marked with black, as old Horace [the Latin poet] would say." He rang the plantation bell for the assembly of the Negroes and read to them the law of the plantation about leaving the plantation without a pass. Then he personally administered to Henry, who had violated the plantation law, a whipping of fifteen lashes.

The maintenance of discipline over the slaves was one of the main functions of the overseer, but in 1852 Eppes was very dissatisfied with his overseer because he was not strict enough with the Negroes, with the result that little work was done on the plantation. To command slaves, he observed, the overseer must first obtain their respect, but Eppes's overseer was not respected by the Negroes. Accordingly, he himself had to intervene at times to control the slaves who got out of hand. On one occasion (Sept. 11, 1859) when a slave had taken his white boat and left the plantation without permission, he ordered all "the hands" to be present to witness the punishment of the offender, "finding by experience," he wrote in his diary, "that it exerts a wholesome fear and enables me to get along with very little punishment, which is the most disagreeable thing connected with slavery." When he had constant trouble in 1859 in regulating "Bins," a young slave, he sold him to a Richmond firm of slave dealers, commenting that it was painful to do so, but that it had to be done or discipline over the other slaves would disappear.

Eppes was an industrious and capable agriculturist. He arose early, sometimes at half past four in the morning, walked into the fields to give instructions and see that the slaves worked properly, and he attended to the buying of clothes for the slaves and to the selling of the crops. He was a progressive farmer who read the works of the agricultural reformers, John Taylor of Caroline and Edmund Ruffin. Following their ideas, he fertilized his fields with marl, plaster of Paris, and guano, and he bought up-to-date agricultural machinery; for instance, in September 1852 he bought two Hussey reapers. He was elected president of the agricultural society of his county, Prince George, and he and the members of the society viewed each others' fields at intervals for ideas on improving their own methods of agriculture. On December 4, 1860, he gave an address before the Hole and Corner Club on "Early Agriculture of Virginia."

The many activities required in managing his estates and Negroes left him little time for cultural interests. He mentioned having a piano imported from Philadelphia and lending from his library a volume of Calhoun's speeches and Mayne Reed's *The Scalp Hunters.* His chief amusements seem to have been hunting, smoking "segars," entertaining visitors, and going to church. His social position was indicated by the invitation from Hill Carter of Shirley in 1858 to a dinner for the British minister, Lord Napier, and his wife. That he realized his privileged position in Southern society was also indicated by his mention on July 11, 1850, of his family traditions; indeed, family traditions were one of the formative and sustaining forces of the Southern aristocracy.

Eppes was typical of the old planter class in his interest in religion. He was a low church Episcopalian, a member of the vestry, and a faithful attendant of church on Sunday. Occasionally he attended services at a Methodist church, but he thought them lacking in dignity as compared with the Episcopal church service. He invited his clergyman to dinner, talked with him about Christian unity and the revision of the prayerbook, and on one occasion borrowed 25¢ to put in the collection box on Sunday. He had a strong faith in orthodox Christianity and in immortality, and he recorded his hope to be reunited in Heaven with his first wife, Nina, a Philadelphia girl to whom he had been passionately devoted.

In politics Eppes was a conservative, as was the typical Virginia planter. On November 6, 1860, he voted for John C. Breckinridge and Joseph Lane for president and vice-president because they stood for the equality of the states and the protection of slave property. When Lincoln was elected Eppes advocated the acceptance of the decision unless his administration violated by an overt act the rights of the Southern states. In the election of February 4, 1861, for delegates to the convention called to decide whether Virginia should secede, he refused to vote for either candidate to represent his county. He did not approve of either Edmund Ruffin, Jr., because he had South Carolina ideas of forming a Southern Confederacy, or of Timothy Rives, a "regular politician" who was devoted to the non-slaveholding interests of Virginia and was willing to sacrifice slavery to perpetuate the Union. Eppes defined his position as "Being myself a moderate man in my views," and favoring Virginia leaving the Union only as a last resort. Yet after the firing on Fort Sumter he signed a paper on April 15 instructing the county delegate to the state convention to vote for secession, but he was very sad in doing so, especially since he had friends and relatives in Philadelphia. The excitement and preparations for war that he saw in Petersburg shortly thereafter, he wrote in his diary, reminded him of the Revolution in Paris which he had witnessed during a European visit. When he felt that patriotism called him to arms, his mind was distressed over a conflict between his duty to his state and to his family, for his wife was about to have a baby and his plantations needed his supervision. He showed his patriotism, however, by sending nine of his slaves to work on the fortifications for the defense of the state and he contributed $580 to outfit ten troopers from his county. Ultimately he went into the army, leaving instructions for his Negro foreman Stewart to carry on the cultivation of his plantations, but after fifteen months of military service his health failed and he was discharged from the army.

Despite a general uniformity of way of life and of views conditioned by their pursuit of agriculture and management of slaves, there were great differences of personality, culture, and personal philosophy among the planters. The type of aristocratic planter that developed in hilly and mountainous eastern Tennessee, such as Dr. James G. M. Ramsay, for example, was influenced by different geographic and social conditions than were those that modified the lives of planters of coastal Virginia and South Carolina. Dr. Ramsay, who wrote a revealing autobiography in 1870, was a planter and businessman whose temperament and outlook were aristocratic despite the fact that the region in which he grew up was dominated by yeomen with a very democratic philosophy. Born in Knox County in eastern Tennessee in 1797 when it was a semi-frontier society, he was descended from Scotch-Irish Presbyterians who had migrated to Pennsylvania and thence to the wild country around Knoxville (founded 1791). His family produced enterprising and natural leaders, and young Ramsay was given a good education, graduating from Washington College at Jonesboro, Tennessee, and then studying medicine for two years at the University of Pennsylvania. Returning to his native state, he became a doctor in Knoxville and a businessman as well, and later a planter, whose estate of Mecklenburg was located at the juncture of the French Broad and Holston rivers, where the Tennessee River is formed. He had broad and public-spirited interests that led him to promote the building of a railroad to connect Knoxville with an Atlantic seaport. In 1853 he published a history of pioneer days in his state entitled *Annals of Tennessee*. He participated actively in the civil life of Knoxville, where he was elected first president of its Bank of Tennessee and was one of the founders of the East Tennessee Historical and Antiquarian Society.

He was a strong supporter of the institution of slavery and of Southern interests. In 1858 he wrote letters to Leonidas Spratt, the South Carolina propagandist for the reopening of the African slave trade, endorsing this movement. In the same year he described the growth of sectionalism in the nation as follows: "Our people will never again be a unit. The antagonism is too strong, the estrangement is too deep-seated to be reconciled or healed. We are essentially two people[s]—we are not only not homogeneous but we have become radically heterogeneous—Our passions, our tastes, our character, even our vices are different and dissimilar. Our interests conflict."

He characterized the masses of the North as venal, corrupt, and selfish, so that the proud Cavalier spirit of the South and of the slaveholder "could not harmonize with them in a governmental union."

Doctor Ramsay illustrated (despite his bitter sectional feeling) some of the best qualities of the Southern aristocrat. With an admiration for the Greek and Latin classics, he sprinkled his writing and letters with Latin phrases. Like the colonial aristocrats, he believed in the spirit of *noblesse oblige* and placed high value on family and lineage, showing a contempt for pseudo-aristocracy based on wealth. He had a great appreciation both for the honor of a gentleman and of his region and for chivalric conduct. On his plantation Mecklenburg he founded an academy and assembled a notable library of 4,000 volumes. Although he was called "the Duke of Mecklenburg," his life was far from that of a gentleman of leisure —he declared in 1871 that he had continuously held public office from 1817 to the Civil War and during that period he could not recollect that he had ever been idle a whole day.

Dr. Ramsay was an example of the aristocratic planter who continuously held public office, motivated predominantly by public spirit and a sense of *noblesse oblige*. But in the last decade of the ante-bellum period the great majority of planters devoted their energies to the manifold responsibilities of managing their plantations, confining their public activities mainly to voting, paying taxes, attending militia muster, supervising the work of their slaves on the public roads that ran in front of their estates, and paying small fines rather than serving on the patrol.

The Northerners in 1860 maintained that the Southern states were ruled by an aristocracy, but this is a highly questionable assumption. The political machinery and laws of the Southern states, with the exception of South Carolina, were fully as democratic as those of the Northern states. Professor Fletcher Green in his presidential address for the Southern

Historical Association in 1945, entitled "Democracy in the Old South," Gustavus W. Dyer in *Democracy in the South Before the Civil War,* and Charles S. Sydnor in *The Development of Southern Sectionalism,* have brought forward convincing evidence that constitutional revisions and the change of laws, beginning in the early part of the nineteenth century before the Jacksonian movement and completed in the 1850's, transformed the South from a conservative aristocracy, in which the people participated very little in their government, into a full-fledged democracy of white voters. Professor Green in the address cited above, which was published in the *Journal of Southern History* (February 1946), made comparisons between the Northern and Southern states in voting in the presidential election of 1828 which indicated approximately a similar amount of voting of the white population in the two sections—considerably below 10 per cent—while in the presidential election of 1850 the precentages of whites voting was 16.6 per cent for the South, 17.9 per cent for the North.

Still another type of evidence tends to refute the legend of the aristocratic rule of the South on the eve of the Civil War —namely, the turnover in office holding. Professor Daniel M. Robison made a study of the political careers of the high officials of the cotton states from 1828 to 1860 according to their length of tenure in office. This study was published in an article in the *Journal of Southern History* (August, 1937). He based his study largely on the biographical sketches of some 550 governors, U. S. Senators, and members of the House of Representatives to be found in the *Biographical Directory of the American Congress, 1774-1936* and the *Dictionary of American Biography.* From 1828 to 1860, he found that the average tenure of office of the United States Senators from Alabama, Arkansas, Florida, Georgia, Louisiana, Mississippi, and South Carolina was less than six years, that of representatives slightly longer than four years, and of governors scarcely three years. The Whig and Democratic parties during much of this period were nearly equal in strength, a fact which tended to prevent the holding of public office in the South for long periods and contributed to the more democratic nature of Southern politics.

In 1902 Gustavus W. Dyer, an instructor in economics and sociology at Vanderbilt University, conducted personal interviews with twenty-five citizens of four counties in eastern Virginia who had lived under the old regime before the war, all of whose ages in 1860, with the exception of two, were twenty-five years or above. About half had been engaged in farming and the others were professional men or artisans. Approximately half of the number had owned a few slaves, one as many as thirty; all of them, he reported, said that there existed a good feeling between the big slaveholder and other members of the community, that the wealthy slave-holders did not attempt to intimidate the poor voters at elections, and virtually all stated that the ownership of a large number of slaves did not give a candidate an advantage in a political contest with a poor man.

The active men—the moving force—in Southern politics in the last decade of the ante-bellum period—seem to have been those ambitious men that came up from the ranks, such as J. J. Pettus, governor of Mississippi, "Zeb" Vance, governor of North Carolina, and Joseph E. Brown, governor of Georgia, rather than the wealthy planters. Francis W. Pickens, governor of South Carolina in 1861, who certainly should have known the inner workings of politics in that most aristocratic of the states, observed in a public letter in 1866 that the largest slave holders were generally in favor of caution and prudence in the secession movement, while the small property holders were the driving force. "As a general rule," he declared, "the large slaveholders and cotton planters had little to do with politics, and it was the great mass of the other class [the small property holders] who have ever held a large control over the public opinion of the Southern states."

The political apparatus of a government may be quite

democratic but the spirit of the society may be aristocratic and the actual working of the government far from democratic. One of the most vital concerns of the people was the question of taxation, and in this respect the property of the slaveholder in the South was more lightly taxed than that of the non-slaveholder. Usually the value of the slaves on a plantation was greater than that of the real estate, but slaves were taxed only by a light poll tax and slaves under twelve years of age and over sixty were not taxed at all. The incredibly low amount of taxes that rich planters paid on their land and slaves is illustrated by the fact that General Duncan L. Clinch, a great rice planter of Georgia, with an estate of 5,045 acres, 210 slaves, and two four-wheel carriages, all together worth two million dollars, paid in 1848, the year before his death, a tax of $65.62. At the close of the ante-bellum period there was an unsuccessful movement among the non-slaveholders, especially in North Carolina and Virginia, to tax all property ad valorem.

Furthermore, the slaveholders had an unfair advantage in the legislatures of several states in that representation was based on the federal ratio or total population instead of on the basis of white population. Finally, the control of court-house officeholders or "rings" thwarted the democratic influence in some counties, and family influence continued to be important. De Forest made a penetrating observation about the influence of local leaders in determining public opinion and the way the people of South Carolina voted: "Every community [of the state] had its great man, or its little great men, around whom his fellow citizens gather when they want information, and to whose monologues they listen with a respect akin to humility." In the Greenville District, for example, the great man, or "the central monkey" as De Forest called him, was Governor Benjamin F. Perry, who dominated the proceedings in 1865 of the South Carolina Constitutional Convention.

It was part of the aristocratic legend of the Old South

that the planters were a well-educated class, versed in the Greek and Roman classics, and readers of books. This description fitted only a small minority of the planters who interspersed their writing and speeches with Latin phrases and words, and could quote passages from Homer. Hundley in his description of the virtues of the Southern gentleman does not claim for him the habit of extensive reading, for he recognized that the average planter was a practical gentleman absorbed in managing his plantation and slaves, marketing his crops, hunting, fishing, and visiting. Margaret Mitchell in *Gone with the Wind* sums up the end and aim of Scarlett O'Hara's friends, the wealthy society group, as "raising good cotton, riding well, shooting straight, dancing lightly, squiring the ladies with elegance and carrying one's liquor like a gentleman." In their out-of-doors life reading books, except on rainy afternoons, occupied very little of their time.

Nevertheless, many of the planters were proud of their libraries even if they seldom perused the books—the possession of a decent library was one of the hallmarks of a gentleman. The Scottish M.P., Sir George Campbell, wrote of the planters around Beaufort, South Carolina: "These planters are described as having been very good gentlemen-farmers. They were well-educated, and were specially fond of good libraries." Also William H. Russell, correspondent of the London *Times,* in his diary, April 22, 1861, has described the old-fashioned type of library that the South Carolina gentlemen had in their plantation houses on the eve of the Civil War. Near Georgetown he visited a rice planter's home, noting, "An excellent library—filled with collections of French and English classics, and with those ponderous editions of Voltaire, Rousseau, the 'Memoirs pour Servir', books of travel and history which delighted our forefathers in the last century, and many works of American and general history—affords ample occupation for a rainy day."

A similar taste in the selection of a library seems to have

characterized the aristocratic Virginia planters. The library that John Hartwell Cocke gathered at Bremo might be cited as an example. While a young man he began to assemble a library and he wrote Bishop James Madison, president of William and Mary College, to send him a list of books appropriate for a gentleman's library. The library that he accumulated at Bremo through the years until his death in 1866 well illustrated the observation that John William De Forest made concerning the libraries of the Southern aristocracy in the year after General Cocke died: their "shelves were loaded with the worthy though possibly heavy old books which no gentleman's library should be without." He was fairly sure to own Hume, Robertson, Gibbon, Addison, Johnson, Goldsmith, etc. In theology he was "strenuously orthodox, holding fast by the English fathers in Bible exegesis and distrusting all Germans [the leaders in the so-called "higher criticism" of the Bible] without knowing anything about them. . . . In light literature he was cautious how he meddled with Northern and even with [recent] English publications, lest he should unaware become entangled in some 'isms.' "

Many of the books owned by John Hartwell Cocke remain today on the library shelves at Bremo, but others have been sold. A list of the books in the Bremo library around 1928 was made by P. St. Julian Wilson, a copy of which is in the Alderman Library at the University of Virginia. This list includes more than 1,300 titles of books, a number of titles being sets of books. Of this collection only 37 bore publication dates after the death of General Cocke. There are 124 titles of books published in or before the eighteenth century, including *The Works of Thomas Paine* (1797). Exclusive of Latin and Greek textbooks, there were only 45 titles of books devoted to the classics and ancient history. Rather, the library was heavily weighted with books on practical subjects: agriculture, notably Edmund Ruffin's *Essay on Calcareous Manures* (1832), law, military subjects, medicine, and a surprising number of volumes on foreign travel. General Cocke and his wife were very devout, and their interest in religion is reflected in the over 300 volumes in the Bremo library on that subject, including an astonishing number of Bibles and New Testaments, so that the aristocratic planter and his lady wherever they turned could lay their hands on the holy books, even in the cabinet or the out-house.

Although Cocke apparently disapproved of novel reading, as did many religious people of his generation, the shelves of Bremo contained 27 volumes of Sir Walter Scott's novels, two novels each by George Eliot, Dickens, and Bulwer-Lytton, as well as Fielding's *Tom Jones.* Of American authors to be found in the library in 1928 were Melville's *Omoo,* Hawthorne's *Scarlet Letter* and *The Marble Faun,* Longfellow's poems, the works of Irving, Cooper, and Brackenridge, two novels by "Marion Harland" (Mary Virginia Terhune of Virginia), and Augusta Jean Evans's *St. Elmo.* Besides the books listed above, Cocke accumulated a large number of pamphlets and tracts; a list of those acquired by William and Mary College at a sale at Bremo (in a folder in the Cocke Papers in the Alderman Library) reflects the interests of the master of Bremo in African colonization, temperance, religion, and agriculture.

Very different in tastes and philosophy was the selection of a Creole library illustrated by a list of books in the library of Charles Gayarré, the Louisiana historian. In the Louisiana State University Department of Archives is a manuscript, "Liste de mes livres, faite en 16 Mars, 1829" which Gayarré drew up shortly after he returned to New Orleans from Philadelphia where he had prepared himself for the legal profession. Understandably, a large number of the 875 volumes in his library were legal works. Unlike the library of General Cocke, it contained very few volumes on religion, not even a Bible, for Gayarré was a good Catholic, and religion was not a matter of exegesis or debate. His library contained many of the

Roman classics and translations of Homer by Pope. It was heavily weighted with the works of French authors (twenty-seven volumes of Rousseau, twelve of Corneille, six of Lafontaine, five of Montaigne, six of Moliere, and seven of Voltaire). There was apparently only one literary work of an American author, Irving's *Conquest of Granada,* but his library included many of the standard works of British authors (eight volumes of Shakespeare's plays, works by Goldsmith, Johnson, Pope, *The Spectator,* Bolingbroke's letters, seven volumes of Burke, and twenty-two volumes of Sir Walter Scott). Gayarré was a sophisticated young man of the world, and his library contained works on fine manners, such as Lord Chesterfield's Letters, and on the epistolary art. He aspired to be a distinguished orator and his library contained works on eloquence, including those of orators of classic times, as well as of Bossuet, the great master of French eloquence. Like the Creoles in general, Gayarré had a great love for the theatre, which was reflected in the large number of dramatic works (the largest item in his collection was "theatre francais," forty volumes). Though he was to become a noted historian, his library demonstrated no especial interest in history but a strong interest in literature and a taste for romantic works—Byron's poetry, Moore's "Lalla Rookh," Thompson's "Seasons," Scott's novels.

The possession of a gentleman's library was not the only characteristic of the elite planter class; another distinctive mark of this class was the development of a code of chivalry. It was a manifestation of the romantic movement of the time, expressed in various forms—dress, literature, excessive politeness to women, the holding of imitative tournaments, florid oratory, and a quixotic ideal of personal honor and of the honor of their region. George Templeton Strong, a conservative and cultured New York aristocrat, described in his diary of May 29, 1856, the notion of Southern chivalry held by the upper class of the North and the revulsion against this concept as a result of Preston Brooks's assault on Charles Sumner in the Senate chamber.

"A few fine specimens have given them a prestige the class don't deserve. We at the North are a busy money-making democracy, comparatively law-abiding and peace-loving, with the faults (among others) appropriate to traders and workers. A rich Southern aristocrat who happens to be of fine nature, with the self-reliance and high tone that life among an aristocracy favors, and culture and polish from books and travel, strikes us (not as Brooks struck Sumner but) as something different from ourselves, more ornamental and in some respects better. He has the polish of a highly civilized society, with the qualities that belong to a ruler of serfs. Thus a notion has got footing here that 'Southern gentlemen' are a high-bred chivalric aristocracy, something like Louis XIV's noblesse, with grave faults, to be sure, but on the whole, very gallant and generous, regulating themselves by 'codes of honor' (that are *wrong,* of course, but very grand) : not rich, but surrounded by all the elements of real refinement."

As one reads the diaries and letters of the planters he encounters one of the deepest forces in their lives—a force that supported the medieval ideal of chivalry and at the same time sustained them in their defense of slavery. It was the all-pervading influence of orthodox religion. A vivid insight into the power of religious feeling on the Southern people at the eve of the Civil War is to be found in the manuscript diary and commonplace book of John B. Minor, a professor at the University of Virginia and a member of a prominent Virginia family. He wrote: "When a man was an unbeliever [in orthodox religion] his relatives and friends were terribly fearful for his fate—looked upon him as a condemned man." On July 10, 1858, Minor recorded the death of his older brother Lucian, a professor of law at William and Mary College and a great liberal. Lucian had been a skeptic, but his brother "labored with him" to save him from the fearful brink of

Hell and with delight witnessed his gradual abandonment of his "chronic forms of unbelief and his growth in grace." It was tragic to the people of his generation to witness such a splendid person, an accomplished and elegant scholar, a man of "unaffected modesty and of disdain of those arts which so many are willing to employ to secure notoriety, if not fame," so benevolent of heart, in danger of suffering eternal damnation after death because of his unbelief. But Lucian wrote to another brother "Lanty" (Lancelot) a month before his death that although he had not yet triumphed over his unbelief ("there is a coldness about my heart toward Christ which causes me fearful misgivings lest all be not yet right, lest the belief be not so [clear?] or to increase as to warrant the great Judge or rather King in awarding me a clear judgment of pardon"), he felt that he was gaining ground every day. It was a matter of intellect with him, he wrote; his heart had not been touched or experienced "a new birth." In his struggle to attain salvation his friends tried to aid him with their counsels and prayers, and his brother John read hymns to him (a source for the study of religion in the ante-bellum South that has not been investigated). Finally, a few days before his death, to the great joy of John, Lucian was immersed along with his old friend, General John Hartwell Cocke, a former Episcopalian, and joined the Baptist Church.

The characteristics of the religion of Southerners in the ante-bellum period are vividly illustrated in the manuscript diary of Reverend William Moody Pratt, minister of the Baptist Church in Lexington, Kentucky, from 1845 to 1863. Pratt was a Northern man, born in Madison County, New York, and a graduate of Hamilton College in that state. In 1839 he had emigrated to Crawfordville, Indiana, where he preached and was principal of the Indiana Baptist Manual Labor Institute. In 1845 he accepted a call to the Lexington church despite his qualms over the existence of slavery in Kentucky and "because I would have to battle 'Campbellism'," the followers of Alexander Campbell, who were called "the reformers." He was far better educated than the average Baptist preacher—his diary records that he bought a copy of Niebuhr's Roman history, that he studied Hebrew and French, and that he read a variety of works, the works of Madam de Stael, a history of the French Revolution, a history of China, *Don Quixote,* Scott's *Rob Roy,* Dante's *Inferno,* and Boswell's life of Johnson. He had a conversation with the venerable Alexander Campbell on the merits of Roman and Greek oratory as compared with the eloquence of the Bible. When he preached during his early career in Kentucky he found that the people wished a warm religious discourse, not a cold intellectual sermon, and he adapted himself to their demands. He noted that after preaching to an immense congregation at Covington, "many a tear was shed," and that after the sermon he "retired to the water where I baptized 6." Later he baptized five in "Brother Ajay's pond." He would become so emotionally excited by preaching and his nerves so taut by his strenuous struggle in combating sin and Satan in Kentucky, ("the Devil," he reported, "is attempting to thwart the purposes of God") that after exhorting huge crowds, "every sermon put me to bed." At the end of January 1856, nevertheless, he seemed to be as fiery in his preaching as ten years before, noting, "I had good liberty in preaching—there was deep feeling in the congregation and tears of contrition and tears of joy."

The nature of the religion that he preached can be judged to some degree, by the topics covered in his sermons. On January 31, 1846, he preached on the prevailing sins of the age. This was a subject that fascinated his congregation. On September 20 he recorded: "Preached a sermon of chastisement and opened up the sins of the church and talked exceedingly plain—more so that I had ever done before in the pulpit—resulted in the largest congregation we have had for some time." On other occasions he preached on the evidences of the truth of Christianity, supported by the miracles, on the Holy Ghost, and on the scriptural errors of "the reformers," or Campbellites. There was a strong element of Calvinism in his doctrines and views of life. When he stopped at White Sulphur Springs on a trip to the East in July 1845, he listened to the music of the polka and cotillion, and "saw them kick up their heels," which caused him to have many serious reflections on the dancers' fate "when they should have left forever the gay circle of worldly amusements."

He participated much in the civic life of Lexington, leading a crusade for temperance and the prohibition of sale of liquor in coffee houses in the town, acting as a school commissioner, preaching to the convicts in jail and to the inmates of the Lunatic Asylum. He spent a whole week attending the trial of Lafayette Shelby, one of the aristocrats of the Blue Grass. Shelby had killed a young man who had looked too intently at him and who had, when questioned, refused an explanation. The minister had many things to worry him about his relations with the community—especially he felt the need of caution in talking about slavery, although eventually he succumbed to his social environment and bought several slaves. He wrote, February 9, 1855, in his diary of "the cruel indifference of church members to the wants of preachers" and cited his own case, namely that during the past seven months he had spent $800 on living expenses and had received from the church only $130 in cash, paid in driblets. Also he had trouble with one of his slaves running away and with his female slave having an illegitimate baby and feeling no sense of sin or shame, and he looked with great anxiety to the approach of race week in Lexington for he was sure much wickedness would be committed then. But to balance these tribulations of his life, he rejoiced when evidences of the success of his mission occurred, such as when he baptized "8 ladies," and 1500 people came to see the spectacle, or when at a church meeting, "Orville Parker came forward and made an humble confession of his wanderings and was restored to fellowship."

Although their religion strongly undergirded the life of the Southern people and gave them strength in the first two years of their struggle to win Southern independence, there is evidence that it weakened them in the last two years of the war. As they lost battle after battle, many began to doubt that God was on their side, and this growing conviction may have caused a considerable number to despair and lose the will to fight. The military tradition seems to have been strong among them, but it was directed, to a much greater degree than in the North, toward fighting in the romantic branch of the army, the cavalry. Though the Southerners displayed great bravery and dash on the battlefield, delighting in the charge, they lacked, on the whole, the discipline and efficiency of the Northern troops. Their type of society, based on slavery, made them reluctant personally to take up the spade for entrenchments. Furthermore, the aristocratic class was weakened by the side-effects of the slave institution, exaggerating, as it did, pride and developing a conservative mind and intolerance of dissent. Some of the wealthy Southerners had traveled to Europe or to Northern resorts such as Saratoga or Newport, but in general they were very provincial and either did not appreciate the power of world opinion or disdained it.

Their plantation life tended to make them individualistic, promoting a cavalier attitude toward obeying the law. This latter characteristic was carried over into military life; Catherine C. Hopley, an English woman who taught school during the war in Virginia and Florida, noted that Confederate officers thought little of overstaying their furloughs as well as of resigning their commissions when they were piqued; some of them, such as General Henry A. Wise and Robert Toombs, flatly refused to obey the orders of their superior officers. Despite their faults the Southern aristocracy had resplendent virtues that seem archaic in our industrial society today—their code of personal and regional honor, their devotion to a cause, and their appreciation for chivalric conduct. Maria Louisa Fleet, mistress of Green Mount in Virginia, expressed these virtues in writing to her son in the Confederate army, "I am sure it will be honour enough to tell your children's children that you engaged in the defense of Charleston."

THREE

The Culture of the Old South: Its Greatest Historian

THE OLD SOUTH DID NOT CREATE A HIGH CULTURE IN LITERA-
ture or the fine arts, except perhaps in the art of moving
oratory. It did produce, however, a distinctive Southern culture of great charm in the molding of the Southern type of
gentleman, with his almost quixotic code of honor, courtly
politeness, and his sense of chivalry. Fredrika Bremer, the
Swedish traveler in the South in 1850, has drawn vivid and
perceptive portraits of some of these peculiarly Southern personalities. She visited Joel Poinsett, living quietly on his plantation of White Hall on the Great Pedee River in South
Carolina, after an eventful life of public service, including his
appointment as minister to Mexico. She described Poinsett
as "one of the New World's wise men," philosophical, cultivated, with beautiful manners, and with a paternal attitude
toward his slaves. She talked with James Hamilton Couper
on his St. Simon's Island plantation in Georgia, the owner
of well over a thousand slaves, whom she portrayed as a very

polite man, "possessing as much knowledge as an encyclopedia," a fascinating conversationalist who reminded her of Emerson in his urbanity and grace of conversation, yet withal a very practical and progressive planter. She was charmed with Bishop Stephen Elliott of Georgia, a man of unprejudiced mind, residing in a lovely country estate fragrant with Southern flowers, "an example of the Old Cavalier race." In producing such men—a type that could not be duplicated in the more urbanized society of the North—or in fact, elsewhere in the world—the Old South attained its highest form of culture.

Of the many facets of Southern culture, the one that has been least studied by modern scholars—yet one that reveals much about the whole tone of Southern society is the historiography of the ante-bellum period. If the culture of a society in a particular age has a coherence and an intrinsic unity, it would seem reasonable to conclude that one could gain an insight into the nature of Southern culture on the eve of the Civil War by examining closely an important aspect of that culture, its concept of history.

The greatest historian of the Old South was a Creole, Charles Gayarré, who pre-eminently illustrated the virtues and faults of those Southerners who attempted to write history during the ante-bellum period, as well as the prevailing Southern attitude toward the man of letters. But Gayarré was more than a historian: he was a sugar planter, a slave-owner, a travelled man of the world, and an important political figure. He represented the patrician point of view in democratic, middle-class America. Moreover, he exhibited the best qualities of the Creole planter aristocracy, which was somewhat different, with its Catholic, Latin background, from the planter aristocracy of the rest of the South.

Born in New Orleans in 1803, he was descended from a noble family of Navarre. His great-grandfather, Don Esteban Gayarré, had come to Louisiana in 1766 with the first Spanish governor as *contador real,* or auditor; his mother was the daughter of Étienne de Boré, the discoverer of a process of granulating sugar from Louisiana cane that laid the foundation for the development of the great sugar plantations of the lower South. Besides having a distinguished ancestry, Gayarré was gifted with a brilliant, imaginative mind and a courtly personality. Very tall—six feet, four inches in height—he carried himself with an erect and proud bearing. In 1859, in sending a photograph to a Northern admirer, he described himself as having blue eyes and chestnut hair, and he remarked that the photograph recorded "my features as coarser than nature has given to me." Grace King, the New Orleans writer, has left a vivid portrait of him as she remembered him in 1867 when he was sixty-two years old and she a teen-age girl. "He was," she wrote, "an impressive figure, very tall; our father, a tall man, appeared short beside him; our father was handsome, but the Judge was majestic in his high satin stock that held his head inflexibly erect. He was dressed in a long broadcloth coat and tall top hat. His beard was clipped close to a point beneath his chin." Instead of the long flowing locks that were the fashion of his section at the time of the Civil War, his hair was cut short.

Until he reached the age of forty-eight, Gayarré's life was a success story. After graduation from the College of Orleans he studied law for two years in Philadelphia in the office of William Rawle, the author of a widely used text on the Constitution of the United States, and was admitted to the Philadelphia bar. Upon returning to his native city he was elected to the legislature by an almost unanimous vote. He was appointed Assistant Attorney General of the state and in 1832 presiding judge of the New Orleans City Court, an appointment that caused his friends and associates thereafter to address him as "Judge." While he was in the legislature he showed a liberal side of his mind by strongly opposing in 1831 a bill to expel the free Negroes of Louisiana from the state. Earlier, however, he had demonstrated a conservative tendency in publishing an attack on Edward Livingston's proposed criminal code, partly on the ground that it recommended the abolition of capital punishment. Why Gayarré joined the Democratic instead of the Whig party is not clear, for it would seem that his wealth, education, conservative cast of mind, and aristocratic family connections should have drawn him into the Whig party, the party of the great planters and the conservatives.

In 1835, when he had barely reached the legal age of qualification, he was elected by the legislature to the United States Senate. He was preparing to take his seat in that body when his health failed and he was forced to resign. On the advice of physicians he sailed to France for medical attention and rest and did not return to this country for a period of eight years. When he returned in 1843 he was again elected to the state legislature and showed his partisan sympathies by making an eloquent speech in favor of the legislature's instructing the Louisiana Senators to vote for the annexation of Texas.

In 1846 the governor appointed him Secretary of State, a position that he held for seven years. During this period, he spent much time researching the colonial history of Louisiana and in writing its history. He was responsible for securing an appropriation from the legislature of $2,000 to copy documents from the Spanish archives, and after much difficulty, and with the aid of the historian William H. Prescott, he was able to persuade the Spanish authorities to grant permission for prosecuting this valuable historical project. Also, during the years he served as Secretary of State, he had charge of expending an appropriation of $1,000 a year to purchase books for the state library; his work in this project entitles him to be called "the father of the State Library."

His uniform success in political life came to an end in 1853, and thereafter all his efforts to obtain office were fruitless. In that year he sought an appointment from the Democratic administration of President Franklin Pierce as Minister to Spain, where he wished to continue his studies of Louisiana history by examination of Spanish primary sources. Senator Pierre Soulé of Louisiana promised his support, but at the same time that ambitious politician was seeking the mission to the Court of St. James for himself. When this appointment was denied to him, Soulé secured the place that Gayarré wished, the mission to Spain. Secretary of State Marcy tried to conciliate Gayarré in his disappointment by offering him the office of Assistant Secretary of State but the proud Creole declined the offer.

Instead of accepting a federal post, Gayarré became an independent Democratic candidate for election to Congress. During the campaign that followed he was too high-minded to engage in demagogic appeals to the voters in order to win the election. He refused to be controlled by the regular party organization and denounced it as corrupt and unprincipled. He was defeated, he believed, by corrupt practices. Accordingly, he published a scathing indictment of the unfairness of the election in a pamphlet entitled "Address to the People of the State on the Late Frauds Perpetrated at the Election Held on the 7th November, 1853, in the City of New Orleans." He charged that in this election, one-fourth of the entire vote in the city was fraudulently cast. The foreign-born residents, organized by Senator John Slidell and his machine, Gayarré maintained, had voted illegally; and, moreover, the Irish immigrants, especially, had converted the polling places into scenes of drunkenness, fraud, perjury, and violence.

Such disillusioning experiences caused the proud Creole to lose confidence in democracy. He expressed his views in a work entitled *The School of Politics: A Dramatic Novel,* which the Appleton Press of New York published in 1854. Here he expressed disdain for the crude brand of politics that had come into fashion in Louisiana. So expressive is it of the aristocratic reserve of Gayarré's nature and of his old-fashioned

concept of politics that a pertinent section deserves quotation.
The road to success in Louisiana politics, a character in the
novel asserted, was to ". . . shake hands with every low fellow
you meet—the dirtier the better; dress shabbily—affect vul-
garity—learn to swear as big and as loud as possible—tap
every man affectionately on the shoulder—get drunk once a
week—conspicuously, mind you—in some well known tip-
pling establishment—become a member of every one of those
associations which spring up daily in New Orleans—shout
against tyrants, aristocrats, and the rich—above all, talk
eternally of the poor oppressed people and of their rights—
drop entirely the garb, manners, and the feelings of a gentleman—and you may have a chance of a triumphant election."

In 1855 Gayarré, although a Catholic, joined the Know-
Nothing Movement in Louisiana. This new party in the South
was primarily anti-foreign and pro-Union rather than anti-
Catholic. Many conservative Whigs, their own party shattered
by the slavery issue, joined it. Gayarré, in his temporary abandonment of the Democratic party, was motivated by a disgust
with the corrupt use of foreign-born residents to win elections,
but he was opposed to the rule of secrecy adopted by the
Know-Nothing party. When he attended the meeting of the
National Council of the party, officially known as the American Party, in Philadelphia in June 1855, he was denied a seat
in the Council although the five Protestant delegates from
Louisiana were admitted. He made an impassioned speech
before the Council defending his right to a seat and giving a
Gallic interpretation of the Roman Catholic faith as it related
to politics. He declared that though he was a Catholic, he
rejected the idea that a priest had any control over the tem-
poral affairs of Americans and he ridiculed the fear of some
members of the party that there was danger of the Pope
intervening in American politics. When he was excluded from
the Philadelphia meeting of the party, his Protestant colleagues
left the meeting with him. With their return to New Orleans

the treatment of Gayarré was indignantly reported to an immense crowd in the city, and the Know-Nothing faction in Louisiana refused further affiliation with the national party.

After this unfortunate episode Gayarré retired from active participation in politics and devoted himself to writing the fourth volume of his history of Louisiana. In 1859 he made plans to go to Europe during the following year for further research, and in anticipation of being away for a considerable period of time sold much of his property and bought a small plantation 84 miles north of New Orleans where he could keep his slaves and store his books and furniture. This estate he named Roncal after a family habitation in Spain. The development of the secession movement caused him to give up his European trip, for his sense of honor prohibited him from running away from his native state in a time of crisis. Early in 1861 he made a speech in New Orleans justifying the legal right of secession on constitutional grounds. During the war he resided at Roncal, devoting himself to scholarly pursuits. He invested his funds in Confederate bonds, so that when the cause of Southern Independence failed he was reduced from a position of wealth and comfort to one of penury. His lofty, almost quixotic, sense of honor, and devotion to the Confederate cause led him and his wife to sacrifice some of the debts owed to them in New Orleans because they refused to take the oath of allegiance to the United States after the capture and occupation of the city by Federal troops.

When the Confederate government was established, Gayarré revived his hopes of being appointed minister to Spain. The United States government had honored its writers and historians by giving diplomatic appointments to Washington Irving, William H. Prescott, and John Lothrop Motley, who was minister to Austria during the Civil War; Gayarré had a right to think that he deserved to be appointed by the Confederate government to the Spanish post. He haughtily turned down an inquiry from the Honorable C. M. Conrad at Montgomery as to whether he would accept an appointment to the lesser posts of Berlin, Sardinia, or Denmark, on the ground that "the position would not be sufficiently elevated to tempt me to the sacrifice of my independence and freedom of action." J. D. B. De Bow, the editor of the famous review, promised to speak to President Davis in behalf of Gayarré's appointment to the mission to Spain, but on August 28, 1861, he wrote to his friend, "Your pious labor you have marked out for yourself in Spanish history will I fear be long deferred if it depends on Principalities and powers." He informed his friend that the appointments to be made by the Confederate government would be governed by the same political considerations that had dominated the old regime of the federal government—"party hacks will take the lead of men of letters." On October 28 he wrote pessimistically to Gayarré, "the President does not break loose from the old Party hacks," and thus the historian never received the appointment to Spain that would have aided him so greatly in his historical researches.

De Bow's letters to Gayarré (in the Grace King Papers in the Southern Collection at the University of North Carolina) give indirect and fleeting glimpses of his life and views during the war period. They reveal that at the beginning of the war Gayarré thought that the conflict would be short—a victory for the Confederacy. In October 1861, De Bow wrote that he felt confident that with the coming of winter, Gayarré's health would improve and he would grow strong; "cheer up," he urged, "& go to work again." In December, De Bow commented, "What you say of speculation in New Orleans is true here & everywhere." In February 1862, shortly before New Orleans was captured, Gayarré showed his confidence in the Confederacy by buying, despite De Bow's advice, seven slaves. When the city capitulated in April 1862, Gayarré placed the blame on the Confederate administration and on General Mansfield Lovell, in charge of the defense of the city. De Bow wrote to Gayarré on June 22, 1862, that he regretted to hear of the Creole planter's bad luck with his slaves—"they are behaving badly everywhere," he observed, "thousands desert." Gayarré in the fall of 1863 sent to his friend, who was then the chief Confederate agent for purchasing cotton, an able and lucid exposition on the subject of the cotton trade. In this year also he made a public address advocating the gradual emancipation of the Southern slaves and that efforts be made to encourage Brazil and Spain to do the same in their colonial possessions. As the end of the war approached, in January and February 1865, De Bow's letters indicate that Gayarré was deeply concerned over the evils of speculation in the Confederacy as well as over the necessity to take action on the emancipation of the slaves. To his observations De Bow replied philosophically that the people had come to accept the evil of speculation as a matter of course and that everybody was willing to yield emancipation as the price of independence.

Gayarré shared to a considerable degree the Southern belief that the path to honor lay through politics and not through writing. Nevertheless, in the year 1830, after he had returned from his study of law in Philadelphia, he published his first historical work, *Essai historique sur la Louisiane*. It was largely an abridgement and a translation into French of Francois Xavier Martin's *History of Louisiana* which had been published in 1828. This versatile but eccentric man who had been born in France had immigrated to America, first to North Carolina, and then to Louisiana where he became Chief Justice of the Supreme Court. Gayarré's purpose in publishing this work was to make it available in French to the Creoles. After he returned from his long stay in France he published in 1846-1847 his two-volume *Histoire de la Louisiane*. One of the reasons for publishing this second work in French, he stated in his autobiography, was his desire to preserve the purity of the text of the many French documents that he had included.

In the preface to his first literary volume, *Romance of the History of Louisiana* (New York, 1848), Gayarré has given a charming and witty account of how he became a historian. It was partly the result of chance or accident, which he believed played such a large role in his life as well as in that of nations. The sickness that had forced him to resign his seat in the Senate and had driven him to France, he believed, was the precipitating event in his development as an historian. In the years while he was in France, in order to divert his anguished mind he began to explore the musty archives of France for materials relating to Louisiana. After his return from France he was invited in 1847 to give a lecture before the People's Lyceum in New Orleans. He selected as his topic the early exploration of Louisiana by De Soto and La Salle, and it gave such satisfaction that, upon the solicitation of friends, he published it in De Bow's *Commercial Review* in June, July, and August of that year. During the severe yellow fever epidemic of 1847, he retired to his bachelor quarters, ordered his Negro slave to admit no one, and began to follow up his success by writing three other lectures, the whole being published under the title, *Romance of the History of Louisiana.* He also jestingly explained his decision to compose a history of the early days of Louisiana as a result of ennui, which he could not relieve, as other men did, by getting drunk, for his constitution could not bear any stronger drink than water, nor could he resort to smoking, for tobacco made his stomach feel sick. At the same time he gazed upon the ancestral portraits that hung on the walls of his lodging and they stirred him to investigate and write about the past of Louisiana in which they had been important actors.

In his authoritative study of *The South in American Literature,* Professor Jay Hubbell has observed that Gayarré's *Histoire de Louisiane,* filled as it was with documents, was dry and factual, but that when he began to write in English he changed his style of composition radically and wrote in the popular flowery and picturesque style. This change was primarily due to the influence of Sir Walter Scott and the romantic temper of the times. In the preface to his *Romance of the History of Louisiana* Gayarré stated a sound philosophy of historiography—it was to narrate events accurately, analyze them, and show their meaning. The drawback to this highest type of history, as Tacitus, Gibbon, Hume, and Clarendon had illustrated, was that it appealed to relatively few people. Sir Walter Scott, on the other hand, through his "immortal writings," had shown the way to make history attractive to the general public and thereby had induced many to study the more serious works of history. Gayarré proposed to do for Louisiana history what Scott had done for that of his native land. When history is not "disfigured by inappropriate invention," he wrote, "but merely embellished and made more attractive by being set in a glittering frame, this artful preparation honies the cup of useful knowledge, and makes it acceptable to the lips of the multitude."

In the *Romance of the History of Louisiana* Gayarré presents colorful and picturesque episodes in the early history of the colony from its founding until the dismissal of Cadillac as governor in 1717. He drew vivid vignettes of the leading figures in the colony, pointing out, as did the Greek dramatists in their tragedies, fatal flaws in their character. He entertains by telling of the romantic and sad love affair between the daughter of Cadillac and Bienville, of Iberville's dramatic sea fight during which he defeated four English warships with his single ship, of the strange antipathy of the French officer Richebourg toward philanthropists, of the treachery of the French in their attack on the Natchez Indians, and he even gives a romantic war song of their leader, the Chief of the Beard. He is witty at times, as in his account of the so-called "petticoat insurrection," when the Parisian girls, lured to emigrate to the colony by deceptive propaganda, staged a rebellion because they missed their accustomed white French bread and were disgusted with the cornbread they were forced to eat. His account of Baby, the dancing master, a tall, gangling figure, sitting remarkably erect astride a small mule—a Don Quixote figure—defending himself against a band of Indians with only his knife, the heavy rowels of his spurs, and his terrifying shrieks and finally his routing of them is a delightful bit of comedy. This volume, based on popular lectures, is entertaining and dramatic, but entirely too romantic and ornate for modern taste. He apologized for what he called some slight liberties which he took with the historical record by saying, "I hope I shall be forgiven for having slightly deviated from historical truth in the preceding pages with regard to particulars which I deemed of no importance. For instance, I changed the name of Crozat's daughter."

If Gayarré had continued to romanticize history he would have had no claim to be regarded, as he now is, the Old South's greatest historian. Francis Parkman would not have advised Grace King, when she was doing the research on her life of Bienville, that Gayarré was the best authority in the United States on Louisiana history. Gayarré became a genuine historian when he began to write his four-volume history of Louisiana in English. In 1851 he published the first volume, covering the period from the early settlements to 1742, when Bienville was recalled to France. He made a mistake in including in this volume the 265 pages of the *Romance of the History of Louisiana,* with no changes or revisions. He claimed for the remainder of the volume, however, that "the substance of this work . . . rests on such evidence as would be received in a court of justice." Moreover, he observed, "in the present production, I have been more sparing of embellishments." Gayarré regarded his work on the history of Louisiana as that of a pioneer, and in this view he was correct, for he not only gathered the facts from an examination of the documents, but he also reflected upon and interpreted them in a fascinating prose style.

Gayarré had great respect for primary sources. He declared that he had spent over $30,000—a small fortune in his day—in consulting sources and writing his scholarly history. As he developed as a historian, he based his work solidly on such sources as executive journals, laws, proclamations, letters, governor's messages, and the works of old historians such as Charlevoix and Latour, men who had participated in some of the events which they described. He used these sources critically also, seeking to reconcile their inconsistencies, detect their errors, and interpret them in the light of his experience and of common sense. He was trained in the law and he was a man of the world—experiences which counterbalanced his ardent romantic temperament. His historical writings became progressively more realistic and were clothed in more sober garments than his earlier writings.

One of the fascinating aspects of Gayarré's historical writing is his habit of reflecting on the events of the past and relating them to the present. For example, when the government of Louis XV turned down the request of Bienville in 1742 for establishing a college in Louisiana, Gayarré lamented that Louisiana had continually suffered, from its early history to the present day, from the lack of educational opportunities for its youth. To obtain an education many of them were sent to France or to the North, where they lost sympathy for the peculiar institutions of their native land and returned home with "a much less keen sense of patriotism or state pride." Somberly he observed in the 1860's that he was writing the fourth volume of his history while a general from Massachusetts was a military dictator over his state, and when "Louisianians are called traitors and rebels, when their property is confiscated, and all sorts of outrages are heaped upon them by the sons of the sires who sat in the Hartford Convention, where treason was meditated, but found not hearts bold enough to carry it into execution."

In his account of the battle of New Orleans Gayarré

reached the maturity of his style, free from his former Sir Walter Scott style. His account rests on contemporary evidence and derives much vividness from the fact that he remembered the spirit of the times as a youthful contemporary of the generation that fought the battle. His style is Victorian, with some of the color and ceremonious language of that period—a style much like that of Macauley, Parkman, and Prescott—a literary, rather than the scientific style of modern historians. Nevertheless, his narration of this battle is critical and his interpretation sound in essentials; he attributed American victory to the skillful use of artillery, to the reckless arrogance of the British in their contempt of the American arms, and to the powerful will and military ability of Jackson. Though he is patriotic in the telling of the story, he is no more so than Bancroft; that he could be both critical and judicious is shown in his discussion of the reasons for the panic of the Kentucky militia. He defended his countrymen against the charges that the British made against the uncouth American soldiers, whom they called "the dirty shirts," of waging uncivilized warfare. The Americans were right, said Gayarré, in fighting in this ruthless fashion because their country was invaded, and, reflecting upon the invasion of the South by the Federal armies at the moment of his writing, he exclaimed, "May 'war to the knife and the knife to the hilt' be forever the motto of every Louisianan whenever his native state is invaded."

The romantic spirit was extremely strong in the South of Gayarré's time, inevitably affecting the writing of history during this period. Alexander Beaufort Meek of Alabama and William Gilmore Simms were also good examples of Southern historians. Meek was a versatile and attractive man, an admired orator, and a gifted literary amateur, who in 1857 published *Romantic Passages in Southwestern History*. Simms wrote a filial history of South Carolina in 1840 which continued to be used in the schools of his native state long after his death.

Simms and Gayarré had much in common, and a strong friendship developed between them. Simms reviewed the third volume of Gayarré's history of Louisiana in the *Charleston Mercury* shortly after its appearance and also his biography of Philip II in the *Charleston Courier* in the spring of 1867. He praised highly Gayarré's historical writings as works of art which combined the skill of the orator and the historian. Simms compared him favorably with Prescott and refuted George Bancroft's criticism that the style of the Louisiana historian was much too ornamental for history. Simms acidly observed that unlike the New Englander, the Southern historian was "never dull, cold, stiff, affected, artificial, and that he never takes liberties with his authorities — never perverts them, or for the maintenance of a theory, ignores or falsifies a fact!" Simms thought that Gayarré's style flowed from his ardent temperament and his splendid imagination, enabling him to develop a picturesque and dramatic style. He also claimed, over-generously, a freedom from partisanship in his friend's historical judgments.

Virtually all of the Southern historians of this era, with whom Gayarré should be compared to judge his work in perspective, were annalists or writers who concentrated on narrating events with little attention to interpretation or to the art of writing. Albert J. Pickett's history of Alabama is perhaps the most valuable of these accounts, for Pickett, an Alabama planter, was animated by the true spirit of the historian. In the preface to his history, published in the same year in which Gayarré's first volume of his history of Louisiana was published, Pickett wrote: "Believing that the historian ought to be the most conscientious of men, writing, as he does, not only for the present age but for posterity, I have endeavored to divest myself of all prejudices, and to speak the truth in all cases. . . . So anxious have I been to record each incident as it really occurred, that upon several occasions I have traveled over four hundred miles to learn merely a few facts." He said that he became so exhausted by the labor of reconciling the statements of old authors, toiling over old French and Spanish manuscripts, and traveling through Florida, Alabama, and Mississippi for information, that he had several times almost resolved to give up the arduous task. At the Indian trading post of his father in Alabama, in his youth he had talked often with Indians and Scotch traders. His work has the flavor of authentic contact with the Southwestern frontier, and it has become to some degree an original source for later historians. Yet, he could not escape entirely from bias, for he was an uncritical and ardent admirer of Andrew Jackson. Like Gayarré, Pickett had the advantage of a comfortable income and of considerable leisure, derived from the existence of slavery; he wrote that his occupation as a planter took hardly one-fourth of his time. He is reputed to have had a rollicking sense of humor, but unlike Gayarré, whose writings at times display a delightful play of wit and humor, the Alabama historian when he wrote history was completely serious. A man of indefatigable energy, he worked so hard at his hobby of history that he impaired his health and died in middle life.

In contrast to Pickett's prosaic style, there are certain striking qualities in Gayarré's historical work which elevate it far above the writings of other Southern historians of his period. There is his strong sense of irony, arising from his keen perception of incongruities. A good example of this quality is his description of the sudden change in Jackson's attitude toward the Baratarian pirates whom he enlisted to fight in the battle of New Orleans. There is the vivid and often subtle psychological analysis of his main historical characters, notably that of the Spanish governor, Ulloa. Though he could know nothing of Freudian psychology or that of the recent behavioral school, he shrewdly used his knowledge of basic human nature, which he believed did not change through the ages, as well as his splendid intuitive imagination to understand the motivation of his characters. Free from the psychological theories and jargon of our day, he employed both a keen observation of life and his own wide experience to interpret events. Such attributes have imbued the great histories and biographies of the past ages with vitality and enduring worth. Moreover, Gayarré had the virtue of stating boldly and forthrightly his opinions and judgments of historical events. The Creole historian admired the qualities of bravery, honor — even quixotic honor, such as that displayed by a member of his family, the Grandpré's, in the defense of Baton Rouge — decisiveness, will power such as Jackson had exhibited, and self-sacrificing patriotism. His history, therefore, has a Plutarchian quality.

Gayarré was one of the pioneers in introducing social history into Southern historiography. He sought to describe the feelings, manners, and tone of the epoch which he portrayed. "Battles and great political convulsions," he observed of the contemporary fashion of historiography, "are generally the main features to be found in the historical portrait of a nation, but there are small lineaments which should not be omitted to complete its physiognomy." He proceeded therefore to relate details of the life of the time that other historians had neglected, deeming them unworthy of the dignity of their craft. He cited, for example, the inventories made of the property of the twelve Creole leaders involved in the rebellion of 1769 against the Spanish rule as evidence of the Spartan simplicity that prevailed in the colony at that time. The bedroom of Madame Villere, wife of one of the leaders and of distinguished ancestry and high social position, was furnished with a cypress bedstead six feet long and three feet wide, a mattress of cornshucks and one of feathers on top, a bolster of cornshucks, a coarse counterpane, six chairs of cypress wood with straw bottoms, and some candlesticks holding homemade wax candles. The house, commented Gayarré, was an unpainted little wood structure that looked like an Acadian house of his own time, and Villere's plantation was not large, cultivated by only thirty-two slaves of both sexes and of all ages. Yet living in these unpretentious houses were fine ladies and gentlemen, with the polished manners of the court of Louis XV.

He related some traditions handed down from the time of

Don Alexandro O'Reilly, who suppressed the Creole rebellion, of the refusal of some of the confiscated slaves of the leaders of the rebellion to serve O'Reilly, the executor of their masters. "If these anecdotes are true," wrote Gayarré, "they show that Negroes are capable of heroic attachment for those that hold them in bondage," and he cited also the case of the high-spirited black slave Jeannat, who cut off his own arm rather than serve as the hangman of the colony. Gayarré had one advantage over the modern historian who has to rely wholly on documents and recorded evidence. As Grace King pointed out in her essay on Gayarré in the introduction to the 1903 edition of the *History of Louisiana,* he was associated with the leaders and the old French and Spanish families, he had a wonderful memory, and he preserved historic traditions in his account of the past.

As Gayarré surveyed the French administration of her colonies in the New World, he observed that France had been the least successful of the Great Powers of Europe in establishing colonies, and he tried to account for her failure. Bad economic policy was partly the cause; for example, the colonists were prohibited from exporting crops that would compete with those of French farmers, and their exports were insignificant quantities of indigo, deer skins, lumber, and naval stores. He placed his finger on the real cause of failure — namely that the civil and military officers, as well as the colonists, with the exception of the German settlers that John Law sent over in 1722, never looked upon Louisiana as a *home*. The officers tried to make as much money as possible while they were in the colony, "in order to return, with increased honors, or with ampler means of enjoyment to their cherished native country, to the beautiful France, that they could not forget."

In an article entitled "Charles Gayarré, Louisiana's Literary Historian" in the *Louisiana Historical Quarterly,* April, 1950, Wilfred B. Yearns, Jr., has pointed out the faults of Gayarré as a historian. He accuses him of being pro-Spanish in the interpretation of colonial Louisiana history, of plagiarism from the history of Francois Xavier Martin, of neglecting institutional history, of failing to record quotations exactly, and of exhibiting the characteristics of the romantic and literary writer instead of those of the serious and well-trained historian. Gayarré was a self-taught historian who greatly admired the narrative style of his contemporary, William H. Prescott, and he displayed, according to our modern scientific standards of historiography, some serious blemishes. He included in his history, for example, long extracts from the documents that he had collected with such great effort. But he defended his practice as giving the authentic flavor and spirit of the times. His inclusion of the twenty-six page report of the Spanish Capuchin, Father Cirilo, to the Bishop of Havana in 1772 on the derelictions of the French clergy under the leadership of "the good Father Dagobert," whose main principle in life was to avoid trouble, gives such a vivid picture of the Catholic church in Louisiana that a generalized account in Gayarré's words would have been less effective. He was proud also of having acquired through a paid researcher copies of letters in the Spanish archives that Governor Miro wrote to the Spanish government revealing that General James Wilkinson offered to betray his country for Spanish gold and conspired to detach Kentucky and Ohio from the American confederation and deliver them to Spain. Accordingly, Gayarré quoted long extracts from these letters in his third volume.

Despite his faults, Gayarré's virtues as a narrative historian are so distinguished that his work is still important in the development of Southern historiography. John Spencer Bassett in his study of *The Middle Group of American Historians* adjudged him to have been the most gifted of Southern historians. George Bancroft, to whom Gayarré dedicated the third volume of his Louisiana history in 1854, accorded him high praise. To Evert A. Duyckinck, the New York literary man and editor, he wrote on February 10, 1855, "I should have been glad to have said more and more publicly about this work, and am willing anywhere to be quoted as bearing testimony to its ability, interest, importance, thorough research, and qualities that make a history valuable and distinctive."

Gayarré had an independent spirit and a high conception of the duty of the historian to record truth. In 1866 when the four volumes of his history of Louisiana were published as a set by a New York publisher, the publisher and Duyckinck, who was reading the manuscript for the press, expunged certain passages that they thought would hinder the sale of the volumes in the North. Gayarré demanded that the expunged passages be restored, writing to Duyckinck that he would not for the sake of personal profit (and he was desperately poor then) "consent to sacrifice the enunciation of historical truths." He realized the existence of what he described as the morbid state of public opinion in the Northern and Western states which made it prudent to omit the objectionable passages from his book, but he proudly declared that, "such men as you and I should not be influenced by such considerations. The curse of our country is that no one dares to speak the truth when it runs counter to popular ideas and prejudices."

Gayarré's proud and independent spirit was shown in small as well as large matters. In the summer of 1860 while he was in the North, he wrote to De Bow that he would avoid Saratoga, where he "would meet all the snobs of the U. S. at the heels of the Prince of Wales" [the future Edward VII, who was then visiting the United States]. He seems, nevertheless, to have been influenced by the opinion of his section in valuing, as Edward Socola in his manuscript biography of Gayarré points out, the prestige of holding public office more than that of obtaining the reputation as a writer. In 1857 William Gilmore Simms in a letter thanking Gayarré for sending him a copy of his pamphlet, a *Sketch of General Jackson; by Himself,* warned him against seeking political office and advised him to write history, otherwise he would, like Macbeth, banish sleep from himself. But Gayarré could never, until he was quite old, give up his ambition for the honor and the prestige of office; he hoped to play the dual role, as did Bancroft, of a political figure and a historian.

Gayarré wrote his history of Louisiana at a time when three great Northern historians were writing: George Bancroft, William Hickling Prescott, and Francis Parkman. Their reputations have endured to this day but Gayarré is known only to specialists. In writing history they had certain advantages over the Southern historian. They composed their histories in a favorable environment of scholars and educated persons who could appreciate and aid them; they were surrounded by good libraries, had easy access to publishers, and there existed a ready market in the North for their books. Gayarré, on the other hand, wrote in a society that did not really appreciate scholars and writers; he had to go North to talk with his peers in the scholarly world — with James Parton, the biographer of Jackson, who read the proof sheets of volume three, *The Spanish Domination,* with Bancroft, and with Evert A. Duyckinck, editor of *A Cyclopaedia of American Literature;* he had to make expensive journeys to New York to negotiate with publishers, and to Washington to consult the State Department Archives, especially to study the papers of the first territorial governor of Louisiana, W. C. C. Claiborne. After the Civil War, when Southerners were too poor to buy books, he had a slim market for his literary productions. In 1860 he founded the Louisiana Historical Society in New Orleans, chartered by the state, and for twenty-eight years he was president. However, in 1888 he resigned, despondent over lack of interest in the history of the state and the failure during this long period to get a cent of money from the state government for the society.

Of the three distinguished Northern historians that were contemporaries of Gayarré, the one that offers the most striking similarities and contrasts is Francis Parkman. Both men were born in affluence, and their inherited wealth made their writing of history easier. But the Civil War swept away Gayarré's fortune while Parkman continued to enjoy financial security to the end of life. Both had a distinguished ancestry and a patrician point of view. Both suffered tremendously from ill health. Parkman was the greater sufferer, so that for long periods he was incapacitated by an extreme nervous ailment and by failing eyesight. He overcame these handicaps so courageously and with such resolute will that his biographer, Mason Wade, has entitled his study of him, *Francis Parkman, Heroic Historian*. Both historians wrote about the French colonists in America, but Parkman painted on a larger canvass than Gayarré the epic struggle of the English and the French to win a continent. Parkman had the advantage, too, in knowing the background of the American wilderness and of having studied the American Indian first-hand; as a young man he had made a trip along the Oregon Trail and had lived for a while with Sioux Indians. On the other hand, Gayarré had a deeper understanding of the French colonists and of the Catholic priests; he had associated with the historic families of Spanish and French descent in Louisiana as well as those in Spain and France, and he had absorbed their traditions. Both historians studied the primary sources deeply, Parkman, however, the more critically, and they both had a splendid historic imagination and a flair for dramatic narration. Dominated by an aristocratic bias, both men paid little attention to the prosaic lives of the common people, but concentrated on drawing the portraits and describing the actions of the leaders. In so doing they were fond of using the device of antithesis and contrast, and consequently they often failed to recognize the powerful economic and social forces that largely determined the actions and policies of the leaders.

Gayarré was eighteen years older than Parkman, but the latter, although he had dallied with the study of law like Gayarré, had resolved in college to make history his pursuit.

Illness prevented Parkman from publishing until 1851 but his first historical study, *History of the Conspiracy of Pontiac,* was a masterpiece which demonstrated his graphic and brilliant historical style. In that year Gayarré published the first volume of his *History of Louisiana,* which was an amateur work, not equal in credibility, critical ability, and profundity to the work of the younger scholar. Parkman did not publish his second historical volume, *Pioneers of France in the New World,* until 1865, a year before Gayarré published the last volume of his magnum opus. After finishing this volume Gayarré declined in historical scholarship and wrote nothing significant. Desperately poor, he turned to writing unsuccessful novels and articles to support himself. During these sad years for the Louisiana historian, Parkman, despite his many physical ailments, continued to grow in stature as a historian, publishing his last work, *A Half Century of Conflict,* in 1892, the year before his death and four years before Gayarré died.

Gayarré was a different sort of American aristocrat than Parkman's Brahmin patrician. Parkman thought that the South was ruled by an oligarchy of slaveholders; Gayarré regarded the Yankees as a cold, materialistic people. The two men agreed, however, that the Negro constituted an inferior race; but Parkman thought that Anglo-Saxons were superior to the Latin people, while Gayarré recognized the virtues of the French and Spanish. Gayarré, the Democrat, and Parkman, the Whig, believed that the elite should rule, and both wrote their histories with the conviction that leaders were the determining forces of history. Exhibiting some of the faults of the Creole society which had formed him, Gayarré could well have used some of the Yankee thrift and concern for money that he disdained, for, as Grace King observed, he was no financier and allowed his own fortune and that of his wife to slip through his fingers. Although after the Civil War he supported the campaign of George Washington Cable to reform the penal system of the South and he sought to eliminate corruption in politics both in the Old and the New South, he was essentially a conservative, reasonably content with the status quo of 1860, the old regime.

Moreover, a different sense of values distinguished Gayarré and the Creoles from Parkman's New Englanders, and even from the Southern planters of Anglo-Saxon heritage. The Creole historian had a Gallic wit as well as the hedonistic nature of the Creole that was lacking in Parkman's histories. He did not scorn the pleasures of this world, nor was he a moralist as was Parkman in writing history. In a charming essay about his boyhood on the Boré plantation, entitled "A Louisiana Sugar Plantation of the Old Regime," Gayarré portrayed some of the virtues of aristocratic Southern society that passed away after the Civil War. He described the fine manners, the courtliness, the loyalty to family, the paternal attitude toward the slaves, the chivalry shown, especially to women, the hospitality of the Southern people, and the trust that existed among gentlemen based on the prevalance of a high sense of honor. Gayarré was the *beau ideal* of the Creole aristocracy, which regarded culture as including something more than education in books, an art of life that took account of the value of leisure, of good conversation, of the love of nature, and of the breeding of a gentleman.

When William H. ("Bull Run") Russell, the London *Times* correspondent, visited several of the Louisiana plantations in 1861, he made some perceptive observations of the differences between the Creole and the Anglo-American planters. He visited the plantation of the Creole Ex-Governor Roman, who met him with great courtesy at the levee and conducted him through the garden to the mansion. Russell commented: "The French Creoles love gardens; the Anglo-Saxons hereabout do not much affect them, and cultivate their crops up to the very doorway." The English visitor also noted: "It was curious to observe so far away from France so many traces of the life of the old seigneur — the early meals, in which supper took

the place of dinner — frugal simplicity — and yet a refinement of manner, kindliness, and courtesy not to be exceeded."
He reported that, according to universal repute, the Creoles
were kinder and better slave-masters than the native Americans, and he saw evidence of a paternalistic regard for the
slaves on Governor Roman's plantation; the Governor permitted his slaves, contrary to the custom of Anglo-Saxon
masters, to dance every Sunday to the accompaniment of the
fiddle in the sugarhouse. Russell drew a portrait of a wealthy
Creole planter, Monsieur Potier, brother-in-law of Roman,
who very kindly entertained him on his plantation: "He is a
grave, earnest man with a face like Jerome Bonaparte, and a
most devout Catholic; and any man more unfit to live in any
sort of community with English Puritans one cannot conceive;
for equal intensity of purpose and sincerity of conviction on
their part could only lead them to mortal strife." His house
had the appearance of a French chateau "erected under trop-
ical influences," with a beautiful garden laid out with con-
servatories, orange trees, and date-palms, and ponds full of the
magnificent Victoria Regina in bloom. A firm believer in states'
rights, he had no conception of the economic power of the
North or the determination of the people to put down secession.

In contrast to the Creole gentlemen, some of whom were
educated in France, the Anglo-American planters were hard-
driving businessmen like the richest planter in Louisiana, John
Burnside, or planters like Duncan Kenner, who was a sporting
man, fond of his racing stable. The Creoles, Russell observed,
did not show any great enthusiasm for horse-racing, but he
thought that it was more remarkable "that they do not stand
prominently forward in the State Legislature, or aspire to high
political influence and position, although their numbers and
wealth would fairly entitle them to both. The population of
small settlers, scarcely removed from pauperism, along the
river banks, is courted by men who obtain larger political

influence than the great land-owners, as the latter consider it beneath them to have recourse to the arts of the demagogue." Nevertheless three Creoles, Mouton, Roman, and Hébert, served as governors of the state of Louisiana before the Civil War.

Like the South Carolina rice planters, the Creole planters had easy access to a sophisticated city, and many of them had city residences as well as their plantation homes. Grace King in her admirable volume, *Creole Families of New Orleans,* has described some of the Creoles prominent in the life of the city, notably Bernard de Marigny, political leader of the Creoles, who at his estate Fontainebleau entertained lavishly, as did some of the leaders in business. Such was Edmond Forstall, who was both business man—the representative from 1832 to 1872 of Baring Brothers and of Hope and Co.—and the owner of a sugar plantation. He was an example of the merchant-patrician of New Orleans on the eve of the Civil War, distinguished for his polished manners, a patron of the opera and theater, a dilettante of the fine arts, a linguist, and a shrewd financier who saved his fortune from the wreck of the Civil War. On the other hand, the remarkable manuscript diary of Lestant Prudhomme, son of a Creole planter of the Natchitoches region, reveals some of the characteristics developed by the Creoles living on lonely plantations isolated from the exciting life of a gay city. While the masses of the Creoles were an ignorant, indolent, and pleasure-loving folk, the Creole aristocrats—as proud of their lineage from France and Spain as the "F.F.V.'s" of Virginia are of their descent from so-called "Cavaliers," or the English squirearchy—developed a charming family life and a unique culture. The passing of this culture and way of life—*the ancien regime*—that Gayarré exemplified and which the Civil War and Reconstruction largely destroyed will be described in the following chapters.

FOUR

What Happened to Culture in the Confederacy

THE FOUNDING OF THE SOUTHERN CONFEDERACY, YOUNG Sidney Lanier predicted, would inaugurate a new and glorious era of culture in the Southern states. Having freed themselves from the galling bondage of the old Union, the Southern states would experience a rejuvenation, a sudden burst of prosperity and culture. Macon, Georgia, his birthplace, would become an art center, its streets lined with marble statues like those of classical Athens. This vision of the creation of a great cavalier republic was not simply the fantasy of an imaginative young Southerner; ten years before, the mature statesman Langdon Cheves in a speech at the Nashville Convention urging the Southern states to secede, had grandiloquently declared: "Unite and you shall form one of the most splendid empires on which the sun ever shone. . . ." In a like spirit Henry Timrod in his poems "Ethnogenesis" and "The Cotton Boll" envisaged a glorious future for the newborn republic. It is quite possible that had the Southern Confederacy won its independence this dream might have been partially realized, resulting in a flowering of literature such as Ireland experienced after obtaining its independence.

Whether a renaissance of letters and art would occur in the Confederacy as a result of independence depended largely on whether the threatening war should be short and glorious, or a long conflict of attrition. In 1861 Southerners as a whole anticipated with great confidence that the war which had started would be a short one. J. D. B. De Bow, the editor of the famous *De Bow's Review,* wrote to his friend, Charles Gayarré on July 4, 1861, "I agree with you the war cannot last long — we can beat them on every field when they no not outnumber us more than 3 to 1." A month later he assured Gayarré: "One other such battle [as Bull Run] and peace on our terms." Today, we can only be amazed at the low opinion most Southerners had of the North, and conversely of their romantic faith in the power of the Southern spirit and the gallantry of the people to prevail over the enormous superiority of the enemy in physical resources and manpower.

Their illusion of superiority extended to the point of believing that the level of Southern culture was much higher than that of the North, which they had stereotyped as grossly materialistic. Southerners prided themselves in a belief that they excelled the Yankee in all of the finer points of civilization: gracious manners, genuine hospitality, chivalry, gallantry in war, the refinement and taste of their aristocracy, the enjoyment of leisure, a harmony with nature, the art of conversation, and the high sense of honor of its people. Mrs. Gertrude Thomas, who lived on a plantation near Augusta, commented in her diary in December 1863 (MS in Duke University Library) on the elegance of manners possessed by Southern gentlemen. They acted, she wrote, as though they were to the manor born, displaying great poise and lack of self-consciousness in meeting people and in conversing. But William H. Russell, the London *Times* correspondent during the Civil

War, was impressed by a peculiarity of Southern manners that did not please him. When he met Southern gentlemen, in contrast with Englishmen, they shook his hand vigorously and seemed very warm-hearted and friendly, but after this ceremony was over, they went on their way with apparent indifference.

The anti-intellectual nature of Southern society on the eve of the Civil War did not provide a favorable climate of opinion in which to attain Sidney Lanier's vision. The literary man, the artist, and the teacher were not appreciated. This attitude is especially reflected in J. H. Ingraham's account of the status of the teacher in Mississippi (he himself was a New England teacher in the South). "Teaching here," he wrote in *The Sunny South; or a Southern at Home,* "is looked upon as a trade, both in males and females. For a Southern lady to teach as a governess, she loses caste with many, though not of course, with the sensible and right-minded. I know a lady with two grown daughters who has a school not far from Vicksburg, who will not let her daughters assist her in teaching, lest it should be an obstacle in the way of their marrying *en regle.* This woman understands the character of the people. Now in New England teaching is regarded directly the reverse. Our teachers there are part of the 'respectability' of society. Our professors are aristocrats. Some of our first ladies have been teachers when girls. In a word, a New England mind can scarcely comprehend how teaching youth can be looked upon as a lowering vocation."

Though urban centers are frequently the nurseries of literature and artistic culture, those few cities that the Confederacy did possess proved to be unfavorable environments during wartime for the growth of culture. J. D. B. De Bow wrote to his friend Gayarré, in August 1816, that Richmond was filled with dense crowds (its population quadrupled during the war years); there were no hotel accommodations available; ice was lacking to cool mint juleps; the water was bad; speculators abounded; the visitor was "cheated in every way in expenditures," and a hectic atmosphere prevailed. Nashville was captured early by the Federal armies and its loss struck a heavy blow against one avenue to culture, for it possessed a large stereotype foundry that was desperately needed by Confederate printers and publishers *(Southern Illustrated News,* October 4, 1862). The citizens of Charleston, South Carolina, lived constantly under military threat and at times under bombardment. New Orleans was an occupied city after Farragut and Ben Butler captured it in April 1862.

A hectic gaiety and excitement animated the cities and towns of the Confederacy. The citizens acted as though they must seize the pleasure of the moment, for tomorrow one may die. George Anderson Mercer, a young lawyer of Savannah and a Princeton graduate, wrote on February 2, 1861, in his diary (MS in the Southern Collection of the University of North Carolina) that an epidemic of marriages was occurring in the city, and a week later he recorded that he himself had succumbed to the epidemic by engaging himself to "a gentle creature." All over the Confederacy people were dancing far into the night, young men were serenading the girls; entertainments, balls, and amateur theatricals were being held to raise money for patriotic and charitable purposes.

Eliza Andrews, visiting in Albany, Georgia, wrote on January 27, 1865, in her journal: "the party [at Mrs. Westmoreland's home] was delightful. Albany is so full of charming refugees and Confederate officers and their families that there is always plenty of good company, whatever else may be lacking. I danced three sets with Joe Godfrey, but I don't like the square dances very much. The Prince Imperial is too slow and stately, and so complicated that the men never know what to do with themselves. Even the Lancers are tame in comparison with a waltz or a galop. I love the galop and the *Deux Temps* better than any. We kept it up till two o'clock in the morning, and then walked home." Returning home to the village of Washington a week later, she was rehearsing for tableaux and theatricals, particularly a scene from Thomas Moore's highly romantic "Lalla Rookh." On April 10 while Richmond was being evacuated, she rehearsed with a tableaux club in Cuthbert, Georgia, and went serenading with a party, but she did not attend a performance of the play *Richelieu* by the Cuthbert Thespian Corps because she was keeping Lent.

But Eliza Andrew's participation in gay parties, dances, amateur theatricals, and serenades contrasted with the rather bleak life of perhaps most Confederate girls. Their outlook is reflected in the diary of Emma LeConte, the daughter of Professor Joseph LeConte. When the war began Emma was thirteen and seventeen when near its close she commented on the years of deprivation that the war had imposed on young people. She noted that, instead of attractive clothes, she was wearing unbleached, homespun underclothing, coarser than that given to the slaves before the war, that she herself knitted her stockings, and that her dresses consisted of two calico ones, a homespun one of black and white plaid, and an old delaine of prewar times, and that, although the LeConte family in Columbia, S. C., had more to eat than most of the people, they had only two meals a day, the dinner, usually composed of a very small piece of beef, a few potatoes, a dish of hominy and corn pone, with never any sweet things, even rarely molasses candy. Surveying the past four years of her life, she wrote: "I have seen little of the light-heartedness and exuberant joy that people talk about as the natural heritage of youth. It is a hard school to be bred up in and I often wonder if I will ever have my share of fun and happiness. If it had not been for my books, it would, indeed, have been hard to bear. But in them I have lived and found my chief source of pleasure."

In Richmond J. B. Jones, the rebel war clerk, noted in his diary on September 30, 1863, that though half of the people of Richmond were half-fed and half-clothed, the quantity of produce in the markets was large and of good quality. In contrast to the general deprivation, elaborate dinner parties continued to be held. Mrs. Chestnut of South Carolina attended such a party, given by the Conscription Chief, General John Preston, December 25, 1863, at which oyster soup, roast mutton, ham, boned turkey, wild duck, partridge, plum pudding, sauterne, Burgundy, sherry, and Madeira were served. Such luxury caused her to exclaim in her diary, "there is life in the old land yet." Two weeks later, the English cavalry officer, Fitz-Gerald Ross, recorded in his travel journal, published as *A Visit to the Cities and Camps of the Confederate States,* that although the Confederacy was supposed to be starving, he had enjoyed a capital dinner with Major von Borcke at the "Oriental Saloon" in Richmond. The menu included an astonishing array of good food: terrapin, oysters, turtle, venison steaks, roasted turkey, beef, lamb, veal, goose, various kinds of fish, a variety of vegetables, partridges, robins, snipe, plover, woodcock, *pure* coffee and *pure* tea at $3.00 a cup, various liquors and wines, and champagne at $50.00 a bottle.

Along with the gaiety and the good living at the capital of the Confederacy for a few, which Thomas Cooper DeLeon has described so vivaciously in his *Four Years in Rebel Capitals,* there were bread riots by poor women and a tremendous rise of speculation and war profiteering. *Southern Punch* of Richmond on October 3, 1863, carried the report of a speech by the governor-elect of Virginia, William ("Extra Billy") Smith, in which he bitterly assailed the speculators and extortioners, and called the capital of the Confederacy a modern "Sodom and Gomorrah." The diary of J. B. Jones is full of notices and criticisms of the great evil of speculation, which contrasted harshly with the heroism of the soldiers in the field and the sacrifices of the plain people of the Confederacy.

While the desperate war was going on, the theatre was flourishing in the Confederacy, as it had never done in peace time. The familiar phenomenon of human nature avidly seeking pleasure in the stress, deprivation, and doom of war was vividly exhibited throughout the Confederacy. The Nashville *Republican Banner* on December 8, 1861, defended the policy of keeping the theatre open during wartime because of the immense floating population of soldiers and civilians. The editor observed that the theatre "was absolutely necessary" to attract young men away from the "unhealthy dissipation of the grog shops." Fitz-Gerald Ross noted that in Augusta, Georgia, "there is a very good theatre where they play every night." Although the Charleston Theatre was burned on December 11, 1861, in the middle of the season, within three months Hibernia Hall, where the secession ordinance had been passed, was remodeled into a theater and remained open during the siege of the city. Here the Georgia slave "Blind Tom," billed as "the Inspired Musician" and "the Greatest Marvel on Earth," gave concerts, including his own compositions, the "Battle of Manassas" and "Rain Storm."

The center of dramatic performances was the capital of the Confederacy, whose population had been swollen by hordes of soldiers and transients. The regular residents seldom attended the theater (J. B. Jones, although a literary man, does not mention in his detailed diary going once to the theater); but both the Richmond Theater and the Varieties were filled with paying customers, especially by visitors and soldiers seeking relaxation from the strains of military life. The period of the Confederacy, Richard Harwell has observed, represented the halcyon days of the Southern stage. In the first year of the war the Richmond Theater was managed by a former New Yorker, John Hill Hewitt, a West Point graduate who had settled in the South as a music teacher. Hewitt had volunteered for service in the Confederate army but was rejected because of his age. Nevertheless, while he managed the Richmond Theater, he also drilled Confederate recruits. Though the theater was well patronized by the public his job was full of difficulties and frustrations. The best actors performing in the South were Northerners who departed when the war began, leaving only "the fag ends," as Hewitt described his actors, who were for the most part harlots and "artful dodgers." The profession of an actor in this Victorian age of the Old South was regarded as not quite respectable. Hill wrote that upon becoming manager of the Richmond Theater, "I forfeited my claim to a respectable stand in the ranks of Society." When the Richmond Theater was destroyed by fire on January 1, 1862, Hill departed from his uncongenial position to teach music and write plays in Georgia.

The burning of the Richmond Theater did not quench the strong demand in the city for dramatic entertainment. A new and lavishly decorated theater, its interior shining with much gold leaf, enthusiastically described as "a gorgeous temple of Thespis," arose upon the ruins. It was opened with much éclat on February 9, 1863, and a prize poem written by Henry Timrod was read. At the same time the Baptist minister, John Lansing Burrows, expressed the feeling of many sober citizens when he lamented the expenditure of great sums of money to erect a palace of pleasure at a time when thousands of young men were dying for their country. The theater, he declared, was really a house of assignation where the third tier was used as a meeting place for harlots and their patrons. The actors, he ironically commented, kept themselves from the field of battle for "the noble duty of amusing the populace." But finally, in 1864, Congress put an end to this distinguished service of able-bodied actors by conscripting them, a decision highly applauded by the editor of the Richmond *Examiner,* who usually castigated the actions of the government.

The quality of stage productions in the Confederacy was very poor and contributed little to elevating the culture of the people. Shakespearean plays were occasionally performed, but Southern audiences preferred farces, sensational melodramas, and especially the performances of magicians and black-faced minstrels. *The Charleston Mercury,* on June 1863, commented on the editorial page that Mayo del Mage, "the celebrated wizard of the South," had drawn a very fine audience in Hibernian Hall. "As an incident of the blockade times," the editor abserved, "we would mention that in one of the experiments the magician wanted to borrow a beaver hat [the mark of a gentleman's outfit] from the audience, and only one gentleman in the large assembly was so fortunate as to possess the desired article." The most popular plays were *Black-eyed Susan* and *East Lynne,* which the leading Confederate actress Ida Vernon brought with her from London when she ran the blockade into the port of Wilmington. Hastily written war plays, "gushing with patriotism," such as James D. McCabe's *The Guerrillas,* or lampoons satirizing Lincoln, such as William Russell Smith's *The Royal Ape,* and John Hill Hewitt's *King Linkum, the First,* or the farces, *Great Expectations, or Getting Promoted,* and *The Sergeant's Stratagem* were very popular. The two favorite actresses were Ella Wren, called "the Mockingbird of the Southern theatre," and Ida Vernon, the superb mistress of feminine pathos, described as "all heart," yet at the same time a very good business woman. The outstanding actors were Richard D'Orsay, who succeeded Hewitt as manager of the Richmond Theater, and the veteran William H. Crisp who acted in theaters of the lower South. D'Orsay was often the butt of critics, not only because of his poor acting but because of his evasion of the draft.

Abnormal war conditions not only stimulated the growth of the Southern stage but in the beginning promoted the circulation of newspapers and the founding of new magazines. Before the war Southerners had been in the habit of reading the British reviews and Northern magazines and periodicals in preference to the weak Southern magazines, but the blockade and the closing of access to the North gave a new market to Southern magazines. Maria Louise Fleet, mistress of Green

Mount Plantation in Virginia, missed reading Northern magazines so much that she wrote to her son in the Confederate army on June 16, 1863, "I wish you would do a favor for me the next time you go to Richmond if you can — I have still a hankering after northern newspapers, illustrated ones particularly. Books and papers are the only things that I want from Yankee land and England." To supply the void left by the disappearance of English and Northern magazines, several Southern periodicals were started at Richmond during the war. The most enduring and successful was the *Southern Illustrated News*. First published on September 6, 1862, the editor described the magazine as "a high-toned Southern journal containing not a word calculated to grate harshly upon the ears of the most refined and delicate in feeling." At first it flourished so greatly that the twenty thousand copies weekly which it published could not supply the demand and the editor announced that it was necessary to curtail advertisement in order to save paper for larger issues. The *Southern Illustrated News* had on its staff the illustrator William B. Campbell of Savannah, Georgia, who had left his position with *Leslie's Pictorial* to return to the South because of patriotism for his native land. Other Confederate magazines were: *The Magnolia Weekly*, edited by James D. McCabe; *Southern Punch*, a comic magazine; *The Countryman*, a sprightly periodical printed on a plantation near Eatonton, Georgia, by its editor, Joseph Addison Turner; *The Southern Field and Fireside* of Augusta, Georgia; the *Southern Literary Messenger* of Richmond, founded in 1834; and *De Bow's Review*, which was moved from New Orleans before the capture of the city, first to Richmond and then to Columbia. The Confederate magazines had started out hopefully, but by 1864 most of them had expired.

There were many reasons for their failure, but a principal one was their inability to obtain paper and printing materials. As early as August 28, 1861, De Bow wrote to Gayarré from

Richmond that the quality of paper available was "shockingly bad." Gertrude Thomas, residing on her plantation near Augusta, wrote in her journal on July 31, 1863: "We are taking the *Charleston Mercury* — it is an effort to read it distinctly, so yellow brown is the shade of the common paper upon which it is printed." The *Southern Illustrated News* had boasted earlier on December 27, 1862, that it was published on the whitest paper in the Confederacy, with the best ink, and that it had sent agents to Europe to procure printing materials, particularly boxwood which was used in making illustrations. But as the war progressed paper became so scarce that newspapers were reduced to one sheet and finally some of them, such as the Vicksburg *Daily Citizen,* were printed on colorful wall paper.

The history of the Confederate press is so large that instead of generalizing on its history the story of a single newspaper, The *Chattanooga Daily Rebel,* will be told, for it illustrates the extraordinary difficulties encountered by Confederate newspapers as well as their general character and contents. Just before Memphis fell in June 1862, Franc H. Paul, clerk of the Tennessee Senate, left the doomed city carrying the state archives to Chattanooga. Here in August he started printing the *Chattanooga Daily Rebel.* He persuaded General Nathan B. Forrest to release from his staff young Henry Watterson to aid in editing the paper. It became immensely popular with the Western army and attained a circulation of over 8,000 copies. Watterson was a brilliant writer with a slashing, satirical style. The paper vigorously condemned the great evil of speculation, exhorted Congress to tax more severely in order to prevent inflation, urged strict enforcement of conscription, gave the military news, and tried to keep up the morale both of the people and army. Also, like other Confederate newspapers, it furnished an outlet for poetry and humor and contained reviews of recent books. The *Chattanooga Rebel,* for example, on October 5, 1862, published a poem entitled "The

Marylander's Parting Address to His Wife," and the *Southern Confederacy* in Atlanta on January 31, 1863, published a highly critical review of Lord Bulwer-Lytton's *A Strange Story*. The *Rebel* published contributions from the famous Confederate humorist, Charles H. Smith, of Rome, Georgia, who wrote under the pen name of "Bill Arp."

The Confederate government prided itself on the preservation of the freedom of the press in contrast to Northern practice. Lieutenant-Colonel Arthur Fremantle of the Coldstream Guards commented in his *Three Months in the Southern States: April-June, 1863:* "I find that it is a great mistake to suppose that the Press is gagged in the South, as I constantly see the most violent attacks upon the President — upon the different generals and their measures. To-day I heard the officers complaining bitterly of the 'Chattanooga Rebel,' for publishing an account of Breckinridge's departure with his army to reinforce Johnston in Mississippi, and thus giving early intelligence to the enemy."

After Chattanooga fell to the enemy the press and printing materials of the *Chattanooga Rebel* were taken to Marietta, Georgia, where it was located for about eight months. Here Watterson criticized General Bragg, commander of the Army of Tennessee, so violently that the general forbad the circulation of the *Daily Rebel* within the lines of his army. Since the paper was largely dependent on the patronage of the soldiers, in order to save it, it was necessary for the fiery young editor to go, but he secured a position on the Atlanta *Southern Confederacy,* where he had the freedom to criticize the unpopular general as he wished. When Sherman's army approached Marietta, the *Rebel* moved southward to Griffin, Georgia, and after this position became unsafe, to Selma, Alabama, where its press was destroyed in Wilson's raid in April 1865. As hectic as its life was under war conditions, the "movingest" paper of the Confederacy was the *Memphis Appeal,* which fled before the approaching enemy, first to Grenada, Mississippi, then to Jackson, Mississippi, from which it was "shelled out" by the federal guns, and retreated to Atlanta, ending its Confederate career in Montgomery, before it finally returned to Memphis at the conclusion of the war.

Despite the various handicaps produced by the war, the publishing of books flourished in the Confederacy, as it had never done in the South during peace time. In the two volumes of Marjorie L. Crandall (ed.), *Confederate Imprints, a Check List Based Principally on the Collection of the Boston Athenaeum* (Boston, 1955), are listed 5,121 titles, exclusive of periodicals and newspapers, and this compilation is not a complete inventory. Approximately half of these publications were official documents. There were numerous books published on utilitarian subjects, especially military books which were strongly influenced by the Napoleonic tradition, but there was also an impressive list of works of belles-lettres. Richard Harwell has found that during the Confederate period forty-nine novels, as well as twenty-nine volumes of poetry, fifteen songsters, and five dramas were published. No notable histories were written during the war. Edward A. Pollard of the *Richmond Examiner* published four volumes on the history of the war, the first entitled *The First Year of the War* (Richmond, 1862), but his work was so prejudiced against President Davis that it is doubtful whether it could be rightly described as history. David Flavel Jamison, president of the South Carolina Secession Convention, published in 1864 a life of the medieval knight Bertrand du Guesclin; and James D. McCabe, Jr., and John Esten Cooke published uncritical biographies of Jackson after his death in 1863.

The two most important centers of Confederate publishing were Richmond and Charleston, but the latter was superceded by Columbia toward the end of the war. At Richmond was located the largest publishing firm of the Confederacy, West and Johnston. According to the August 11, 1864, issue of the *Index*, the Confederate propaganda periodical edited by

Henry Hotze in London, this publishing house had imported from Europe during the war thirty-two printing presses, and in 1864 was operating seventy-six presses and twenty-five ruling and binding machines, and was employing 344 persons. West and Johnston published more literary titles than any other Confederate publisher. Sigmund H. Goetzel & Co. of Mobile (Goetzel was an Austrian immigrant into the South) was the leading publisher in the Confederacy of foreign works. Since there was no international copyright law at the time, the pirating of the works of foreign authors could be done with impunity.

The literary taste of Confederate men and women was reflected in their diaries, for reading was one of the main forms of entertainment and of culture. The most popular novel in the Confederacy was Victor Hugo's *Les Misérables,* but Sir Walter Scott continued to have many readers among both the soldiers and the civilian population. Augusta Jane Evans's *Macaria or Altars of Sacrifice,* published in Richmond in 1864 and dedicated to the Confederate Army, was the most successful novel published in the Confederacy by a native author (she was a citizen of Mobile). Sallie Rochester Ford, wife of a Baptist preacher of Louisville, Kentucky, also was the author of a very popular novel, *The Raids and Romance of Morgan and His Men* (Mobile, 1864), which its publisher, S. H. Goetzel of Mobile, advertised as "the first Great Novel of this second War of Independence." The novels of Mary Elizabeth Braddon, an English writer, had a wide circulation in the Confederate states; Kate Stone, a vivacious young belle living on Brockenburn Plantation in Louisiana, for example, read Miss Braddon's *The Secret of Lady Audley.* These women novelists especially catered to a taste for melodrama, sentimentalism, and even Victorian prudery.

The more cultivated readers of the Confederacy read mainly the best authors of British literature. George Mercer, the Savannah lawyer, while an officer in the Confederate Army, recorded in his diary the reading of Scott's *Rob Roy* and *Kenilworth,* Shakespeare's *Coriolanus,* Carlyle's *French Revolution,* Dugald Stewart's *Philosophy of Mind,* and Cellini's famous autobiography. During the dark hours of defeat, he consoled himself by reading histories of the American Revolution. The works of the English novelists, Bulwer-Lytton, Wilkie Collins, Dickens, George Eliot, and Thackeray, and the poetry of Tennyson were favorites among the better educated people of the Confederacy. Mrs. Chesnut's diary shows that during the war she read George Sand's *Consuelo,* the novels of George Eliot, Dumas, Bulwer-Lytton, Thackeray, Dickens, *Uncle Tom's Cabin,* Goethe's works, Byron's poetry, Creasy's *Fifteen Decisive Battles of the World,* Clarendon's *History of the Rebellion,* and Banastre Tarleton's *Memoirs* of his campaigns in the American Revolution. While Sidney Lanier was a signal officer in Virginia, he read avidly — especially Tennyson, the Brownings, and the German romantic writers. When cultivated people turned to historical works, they were likely to read Macauley's colorful history, Gibbon's *Decline and Fall of Rome,* the works of David Hume, Carlyle's *French Revolution,* or works on the American Revolution.

The common soldiers who could read entertained themselves, of course, with much less serious or elevating publications. Confederate presses catered to the taste of Johnny Reb by publishing such works as *Uncle Buddy's Gift Book for the Holidays, The Camp Jester,* or *Amusement for the Mess,* and J. B. Jones's (author of *A Rebel War Clerk's Diary) Wild Western Scenes;* a volunteer told Jones that he had read *Wild Western Scenes* twice, and Jones recorded in his diary December 30, 1863, that his impoverished income had been supplemented by royalties from the sale of 5,000 copies of the book. A Mississippi soldier, J. Hardeman Stuart, wrote in his diary, August 14, 1862, that he wished he had something "solid" to read in camp but that he had to be content with Jones's *Wild Western Scenes* and *Hot Corn* (attributed to Solon Robinson), which he described as a dirty book that no lady should ever see. The common soldier could also laugh over folksy newspaper humor, such as the letters that Charles Henry Smith of Rome, Georgia, published under the name of an illiterate yeoman "Bill Arp," or "The Letters of Mozis Addums to Billy Ivins," which the Virginia humorist Dr. George W. Bagby collected from his contributions to newspapers and issued as a book in 1863.

Not only did the blockade virtually stop the importation of books to the Confederacy (although Kemp Battle in North Carolina read Dicken's *Great Expectations* imported through the blockade), but the invading armies destroyed or in some cases stole many valuable Southern libraries. General Humphrey Marshall of Kentucky told Robert Kean, head of the Confederate Bureau of War in Richmond, that Northern soldiers stole his library, which he estimated to be worth $12,000 and sold it at auction in Cincinnati. When Sarah Morgan returned to her home at Linwood near Baton Rouge after the Yankees had pillaged it, she found that every book of any value except Tennyson's *Idylls of the King,* the histories of Gibbon and Hume, and the *Histoire de la Bastille,* had been stolen; Sarah regretted the loss of Macauley's history particularly. The finest library that was burned by the invaders was that of William Gilmore Simms, consisting of 10,740 volumes, which Sherman's troops destroyed. Another notable library that was destroyed during the war was that of Dr. Ramsey at Mecklenburg in eastern Tennessee.

The long war had a disastrous effect upon the older literary men of the Confederacy. William Gilmore Simms wrote to John Reuben Thompson, former editor of the *Southern Literary Messenger,* on January 10, 1863, that he had done virtually nothing in literature for the last two years, "I need leisure, repose, and my wonted conveniences, for composition," he observed. "I need not say to you, also, how much a man of my excitable temperament may be kept from his tasks by the condition of his Country." Simms had been an ardent secessionist and had entered enthusiastically and optimistically into the founding of the new nation and its preparations for defense against an invading army. On July 4, 1861, he wrote to his Northern friend, James Lawson, that he was practicing marksmanship with his Colt revolver and that he was a dead shot with his rifle. He subscribed twenty bales of cotton from his plantation to aid the Confederate cause. His mind was active in planning strategy for the Confederate army, devising new instruments for war, and freely giving his advice. His low opinion of the courage of Northern soldiers, despite his frequent visits to the North before the war, caused him to make a fantastic proposal to General Beauregard, who commanded in South Carolina, of adopting a form of psychological warfare. The general, he advised, should attach to each company in every regiment a band of ten men painted gaudily and disguised as Indians; he specified that they should wear turbans, yellow hunting shirts, and dye their faces red with the juice of the bloodroot. "If there be anything which will inspire terror in the souls of the citizen soldiers of the North," he declared, "it will be the idea that scalps are to be taken by the redmen. Encourage this idea."

The war strains, the responsibility of managing his plantation Woodlands without an overseer, and the nursing of his sick wife and two children who died during the war, sapped Simm's vitality. Death was a frequent visitor in his household; of his fifteen children, only six survived at the time of his own death in 1870. Although he was able to raise enough food for his family and his seventy slaves, he found that it was necessary to conciliate his slaves and keep them at work by supplying them with molasses. His town house had been burned down before the war, and in 1862 the mansion at Woodlands was largely destroyed by fire, though his library was saved. His friends contributed generously to aid him in rebuilding his home, but Sherman's troops burnt the newly built house, and this time his library also. Cut off from the Northern market for his books, he lost his copyrights and plates, which he estimated to be worth $25,000, as well as his annual income of between $1,200 and $1,800 from royalties.

During the war period Simms's only considerable work of fiction was a serial in the *Southern Illustrated News* entitled "Paddy McGann; or the Demon of the Stump." He published some poems in the newspapers and the Confederate magazines. He also gave Dr. Francis Porcher advice on how to use native herbs, vegetables, and weeds as substitutes for medicines and foods that the blockade and the cessation of trade with the North had made scarce or unattainable; some of these suggestions were incorporated in the previously mentioned *Resources of the Southern Fields and Forests,* which was published in Charleston in 1863.

Among the last sad records of Simms's Civil War period was his letter to Governor Andrew Magrath, January 9, 1865, appealing for exemption from the state draft law. He was then fifty-nine years old, ailing and broken in spirit, and he told the governor that he could walk hardly any distance because of hemorrhoids and an enlarged testicle. The burning of Columbia when Sherman's troops captured the town provoked him to publish a moving indictment of the ruthlessness of the Northern conqueror in a pamphlet entitled *The Sack and Destruction of the City of Columbia, South Carolina* (Columbia, 1865).

The war was a great emotional event in the lives of most Southerners, taking them out of their parochial world to look upon a wider and nobler horizon. Accordingly, it resulted in a tremendous outpouring of poetical effusion. It was an age of excessive romanticism and unabashed sentimentalism, which were expressed in the poetry of the time. The editor of the *Southern Literary Messenger,* the realistic and outspoken Dr. George W. Bagby, commented in the "Editor's Table," in July 1863: "We are receiving too much trash in rhyme. What is called 'poetry' by its authors is not wanted." It was too much trouble, he declared, to tear up this so-called poetry. The newspapers were the most available outlet for those souls yearning to express their patriotic sentiments. In the *Charleston Daily Courier* for the single month of January 1862, for example, nineteen poems were published, among which were "South Carolina's Justification to the North," "McClellan's Soliloquy," "The Devil's Visit to Old Abe," and two poems by Timrod, "Katie," and "La Belle Juive."

In contrast to the disastrous effect of the war upon the older generation of literary men of the South, the movement for Southern independence and the excitement of the war had a stimulating effect upon the younger writers. The valor of heroes, the patriotism of the people, and the pathos and tragedy of war provided real and moving themes for literature to take the place of the pallid and artificial themes of the pre-war period. James R. Randall of Maryland in his poems, "John Pelham" and the beautiful song, "Maryland, My Maryland!," Father Abram Joseph Ryan of Norfolk, a chaplain in the Confederate army who wrote "The Sword of Robert Lee" and "The Conquered Banner," Father John Banister Tabb, who served as a Confederate blockade-runner before he became a priest, the Georgia doctor Francis Orray Ticknor in his "Virginians of the Valley," and "Little Giffen," George W. Bagby in "The Empty Sleeve," John Reuben Thompson in "Music in the Camp," and John W. Palmer in "Stonewall Jackson's Way," wrote poems that elevated the Southern cause. In addition to these heroic and martial poems Southerners composed verse celebrating the Southern landscape, romantic love, and the virtues of Southern womanhood. Much of Confederate war poetry was written by women; of the poets whose work was included in William Gilmore Simms's *War Poetry of the South* (1866), twenty-six were women.

The poet who responded preeminently to the stimulus of

the new nation was Henry Timrod of Charleston, South Carolina. Before the conflict Timrod had published a slender volume of poetry that attracted little attention. He had supported
himself by becoming a plantation tutor. Although he had been
opposed to secession, when South Carolina left the Union he
loyally supported his state and the Confederate cause. In
March 1862 he volunteered as a private in the Confederate
Army, apparently reluctantly and driven by ennui, but his frail
health led to his discharge from the service, and he spent the
remainder of the war as a war correspondent for the *Charleston Mercury* and as assistant editor of the Columbia *South
Carolian*. During the war years he wrote decidedly the best
poetry produced in the Confederacy. Most of his themes were
patriotic in nature, such as "Ethnogenesis," which celebrated
the birth of the Southern Confederacy, "The Cotton Boll,"
"Spring," (the effect of the war in disturbing the beauty of
the Southern spring), "A Cry to Arms," and the noble "Ode
to the Confederate Dead." The North Carolinian, Walter
Hines Page, who became editor of the *Atlantic Monthly*,
wrote that Timrod would have been another poet like Edgar
Allan Poe, composing in a dream world, had not the Civil
War come. Timrod's poetry, Page thought, "portrayed the
spirit of the Southern people in war-time more truly than
elaborate histories can do, and of all the songs the war inspired, there are none comparable to Timrod's."

Paul Hamilton Hayne, a classmate of Timrod in Charleston, illustrated Simms's dictum that during the war it was
the function of the literary men of the South to keep up the
morale of the people. Hayne served in the garrison to defend
Fort Sumter, where he diligently studied artillery practice.
He wrote to his wife, "When I look at the Federal blockaders,
I can hardly keep my temper." In a letter to her on February
28, 1862, he exclaimed, "the ancient poetical 'afflatus' has
strangely come over my spirit again so that I have been composing all sorts of lyrics, chiefly of a patriotic order," and in

April, he commented, "the poetic vein is at a flood-tide." Hayne enobled the Confederate cause by composing such poems as "Charleston," "The Blockaders," "My Mother Land," "Our Martyrs," and "The Battle of Charleston Harbor." In June 1863 he published in the *Southern Illustrated News* a poem entitled "The Southern Lyre," in which he recited the merits of the leading Southern poets, most of whom, he said, had been unjustly excluded by the Yankees from their anthologies of notable American poets. His health became so impaired by military life that he had to leave the army. After his house and extensive library were destroyed in the bombardment of Charleston, he lived near Greenville, South Carolina, where he read literature constantly, studying especially the art of Tennyson and Mrs. Browning, taught his children, and wrote poems for the magazines and newspapers, notably a sonnet in praise of Beauregard. His manuscript diary in the Duke University Library for the year 1864 shows a mounting sense of the doom of the Confederacy and of personal frustration.

Sidney Lanier was able, during interludes in his life as soldier in the Confederate army, to continue his pursuit of intellectual interests. Lanier was an ardent Southerner, who described himself as "a full-blooded secessionist," strongly opposed to fanatics and "Black Republicans." While he was a tutor at Oglethorpe University at Midway, Georgia, he volunteered at the age of nineteen years for service in the Confederate army. He and his younger brother Clifford served as officers in the Signal Corps, stationed at first in eastern Virginia, where he had time to read extensively and to court the lovely Virginia Hankins of Macon's Castle. He acquainted "Ginna" with the poetry of Robert and Elizabeth Barrett Browning, the works of Carlyle, and the writings of the German romanticists, Novalis and Richter. The young soldier had acquired a great enthusiasm for German culture at Oglethorpe University and hoped to follow the example of his most stimulating teacher, Professor James Woodrow, by studying in a German university. While he was in the army he wrote to his father in Macon requesting him to buy at any price the works of Lessing, Schiller, Tieck, and Uhland. He translated Heinrich Heine's poem, "Ein Fichtenbaum steht langsam," entitling it, "The Palm and the Pine" and Herder's "Frühling's Gruss," "Spring's Greeting." His brother Clifford also was enthusiastic about German literature, composing a poem entitled "Goethe's Words." In the army Lanier continued to study the German language, and his youthful letters were interspersed with the expletive "Himmel!" When Federal troops captured his baggage it contained a volume of Heine's poetry, Mrs. Browning's "Aurora Leigh," a German glossary, and volumes of Coleridge, Shelley, and Keats.

Lanier's letters written while he was in the Signal Corps are excessively romantic and full of hyperbole, to such a degree that his father warned him against these tendencies. His romanticism was especially revealed in his attitude toward women; he regarded them as spiritual creatures, and called "Ginna" Hankins and his future wife, Mary Day, "Tube Roses" and "Vestal Virgins." He enjoyed playing his flute, and regarded music as his best talent, but, influenced by the sense of values of Southern society, he repressed for a long time any inclination to pursue it as a profession. While he was stationed at Kinston, North Carolina, he attended on January 7, 1864, a grand tournament, followed by a coronation ball. The tournament was a peculiarly Southern manifestation of the romantic movement that the war did not stamp out. Southern aristocrats dressed as medieval knights would engage in a contest of skill in riding swiftly by a suspended ring, trying to pierce it with long shafts resembling medieval lances. On this particular occasion the "Knight of Dixie" with a helmet made of pasteboard won the prize of the tournament. Southern belles, dressed as queens and princesses, awarded tokens of their favor to brave and skillful "knights."

During his service in Virginia, Lanier delighted in the

popular sport of serenading the Southern belles, especially
Virginia Hankins. Music, indeed, was one of the most valuable outlets for the soldiers in escaping the grimness of the
war. The soldiers sang lustily in camp and on the march, a
recreation that was encouraged by their officers, particularly
"Jeb" Stuart, who had the good fortune to have in his cavalry
the Sweeney brothers, who were skilled banjo players. Classical music was played in the Confederacy, but the enthusiasm
for popular music among the young people was overwhelm-
ing. Even Sidney Lanier, who played classical music on his
flute, wrote home in 1862 that Louis Gottschalk's "Serenade"
was more appealing than Beethoven. Gottschalk, who was
born in New Orleans, was the only Southern piano virtuoso
of the period, and his compositions "The Last Hope" and
"The Dying Poet," were immensely popular. Catherine Hopley, an Englishwoman who taught in Virginia and Florida
during the war and wrote one of the best accounts describing
life behind the Confederate lines, tried to teach classical music
to young girls in a Baptist academy near Warrenton, Virginia,
but she could make little headway against the craze of her
pupils for popular tunes such as "Beauregard's March." Mrs.
Fleet of Green Mount Plantation sent to her son Fred in the
army on November 17, 1862, a list of music and songs to get
for his sister on his next trip to Richmond, a list which included "General Jos. E. Johnston's Manassas Quickstep,"
"Sleighride Polka," "The Golden Mazurka," "Beauregard's
March," "Will You Come to My Mountain Home," a love
song, "Sleeping, I Dreamed," another love song, "Monastery
Bells," "Maiden's Prayer," by Badarzewska, "All Aboard," a
Polka by Engelbrecht, and "Fisher's Horn-pipe." The *Charleston Mercury* of June 17, 1863, advertised the "Never Surrender Quickstep," composed by O. E. Eaton and dedicated
to "the Defenders of Glorious Vicksburg." Music publishing
flourished in the Confederacy until near the end; at least 648
pieces of sheet music were issued by Confederate presses.

The most popular songs in the Confederacy were "Dixie"

and "The Bonnie Blue Flag." The latter was composed by Harry B. Macarthy, "The Arkansas Comedian," and was sung to the music of an old Irish tune, "The Irish Jaunting Car." The lovely Jennie Cary of Baltimore made "Dixie" popular by singing it early in the war to Confederate troops. "When This Cruel War Is Over," and the sentimental ballad "Lorena" were also highly appealing to the soldiers. "Lorena" had such a wide-spread popularity in the Confederacy that Mrs. Chesnut wrote in her diary, "Maggie Howell [the beautiful sister of Jefferson Davis's wife] says there is a girl in large hoops and a calico frock at every piano between Richmond and the Mississippi, banging on the out-of-tune thing and looking up into a man's face (a soldier in uniform) singing that song." Fred Fleet wrote to his mother while he was in the trenches defending Petersburg that he often heard the Yankee bands playing and that "their bands are superior to ours, as the majority of them were formed before the war, and their instruments are much better than any we can procure." But the Moravian Band of Salem, North Carolina, was superior to most of the Northern military bands.

Another form of artistic expression, painting and sculpture, also suffered from the impact of war conditions. Constance Cary Harrison, the wife of Jefferson Davis's secretary, in her *Recollections Grave and Gay,* lists some of the artists of the Confederacy that worked in Virginia, particularly in Richmond. Two of them, William D. Washington, who became an officer in the Confederate army, and John A. Elder of Fredericksburg, Virginia, had studied under Emanuel Leutze in his celebrated Düsseldorf studio. Washington painted the most famous picture executed in the Confederacy, entitled the "Burial of Latané," a captain in Stuart's cavalry who was killed in the famous ride around McClellan's army. John A. Elder painted moving Confederate scenes such as "The Scout's Prize," "The Crater Fight," and "Appomattox," pictures that Mrs. Harrison described as disarming her critical faculty for they produced tears. The painter Conrad Wise Chapman returned from Italy to enlist in the Confederate army and to etch battle scenes. On the other hand, the most notable illustrator of the Old South, David H. Strother, who, before the outbreak of the war, had contributed illustrations and short sketches of life in the upper South in the style of Washington Irving to *Harper's Monthly Magazine,* joined the Northern army, where he served as an officer in the topographical corps. Adalbert J. Volck, one of the 1848 German exiles who had settled in Baltimore, sympathized with the Confederacy and drew caricatures of prominent Northern personalities such as Lincoln and Ben Butler whom he portrayed as "Don Quixote" and "Sancho Panza." He also delineated life behind the lines in his published work, *Confederate War Etchings.* John R. Key, a Maryland lieutenant of Engineers, largely self-taught in art, painted bold and striking landscapes, notably "Drewry's Bluff," where the Confederates repulsed the naval attempt to reach the Confederate capital. William L. Shepperd, who became a prominent illustrator of Southern scenes, and the Chevalier Moses Ezekiel, who fought as one of the cadets of V. M. I. in the battle of New Market, were just beginning their careers as artists when the war ended. Alexander Galt of Norfolk, a talented young sculptor who executed a bronze statue of Jefferson and portrait busts in marble of Southern leaders, died during the war before his art could mature.

Although the Confederacy could afford to suspend its artistic and literary development until victory had been won, it could not withstand the sacrifice of the education of its youth that occurred during the long war. The academies and the "old field" private schools were the principal trainers of the leaders of the South; the public schools in all the Confederate states with the exception of North Carolina and Tennessee were notably inadequate and existed primarily for the instruction of those children whose parents could not pay tuition charges. The closing of a great majority of the academies during the war represented a major loss of culture to Southern society. Some of them closed because of financial difficulties, but the principal reason was that the teachers volunteered for service in the Confederate Army. Such was the case, for instance, in the closing during the first year of the war of Loch Willow Academy in the Shenandoah Valley; its proprietor and principal teacher, Jed Hotchkiss, of Northern birth, suspended his school to offer his services to the Confederate Army, and became the greatest topographical engineer on the Southern side. A considerable number of the Southern academies, nevertheless, remained open throughout the war. In Georgia, for example, some excellent academies continued to teach boys whose fathers could pay the tuition charges. The highly respected Chatham Academy in Savannah, the Collegiate Institute at Athens, and the Augusta Select Academy for Boys and Girls provided instruction throughout the war. Richard Malcolm Johnston, a strong Unionist, resigned his position as professor in the University of Georgia in 1861, and during the following year established Rockby School on a plantation near Sparta, Georgia. Ably conducted and based on the honor system, this school sought to train its students to be gentlemen. In Mebane, North Carolina, Colonel William Bingham conducted the famous Bingham School, also on principles of honor, and drilled his students in military formations.

The disruption of education during the war is vividly revealed in the remarkable diary of Benny Fleet of Green Mount Plantation in Virginia. In the spring of 1861 Benny was attending Aberdeen Academy near his home, but in June the headmaster recruited a rifle company and entered the Confederate Army. For nearly nine months thereafter the fourteen-year-old boy did not go to school. When he did resume his studies in another academy, he had forgotten, he wrote in his diary, nearly all that he had previously learned. His father, a doctor as well as a planter, helped him to learn his Latin lessons, and it is indicative of the strong classical background of a gentleman's education in the Old South that Dr. Fleet found that he could still translate Caesar, Ovid, and Sallust, by referring occasionally to a Latin dictionary. But the good doctor wrote that after helping his son with his lessons, he dreamed most of the night of the declension of Latin nouns and the conjugation of verbs. In his new school Benny studied Virgil, Caesar, and Horace, Latin and Greek grammars, and algebra. The Stevensville Academy that he attended was taught by a young graduate of the University of Virginia who was too frail in health to serve in the army.

Benny continued to attend Stevensville Academy for over a year, while his sister was a student in a girl's school conducted by a minister. She was taught music at home by a German music teacher, a Mr. Ueberwasser, who made his rounds among the plantation families to give piano lessons. He would spend the night in the homes of his patrons and dine with the family. On one occasion early in 1863 during a discussion of the merits of the Confederate cause at the dinner table of the Fleet home, the German teacher expressed some doubts as to whether God was on the side of the Confederacy. Dr. Fleet was angered at the teacher's lack of loyalty and thereupon promptly dismissed him.

As prices continued to rise in the Confederacy and the currency depreciated, the charge for tuition at Benny's school was raised to $50, causing some of the pupils to quit school. Benny continued, however, to attend the academy through the winter of 1864, but the Fleet family had imbued the youth with ideals of patriotism for the South and of the chivalric conduct required of a gentleman, so that he was eager to fight for the Confederate cause. Early in the spring he quit school to drill with a company that was being raised in the county. Procuring a Confederate uniform, he rode away from his home (probably on his horse, "Henry Clay," which he was in the habit of riding to school) to join the partisan rangers of the romantic Colonel Mosby. As he proceeded to Richmond he encountered the Dahlgren raiders, and the bright and idealistic youth was killed at the age of seventeen.

The impulse for volunteering drained a large proportion of the teachers of the South from their positions, not only in the academies, but in the impoverished public schools. Although the first Confederate conscription act exempted from military service teachers of as many as twenty pupils, a high sense of honor, the pressure of public opinion, and probably a desire to escape from an underpaid and lightly esteemed occupation caused many of the teachers to abandon their schools to enter the army. The vacuum thus created was partly filled by women; in North Carolina, for example, the number of women employed in the public schools increased from $7\frac{1}{2}$ per cent to 40 per cent of the total number of teachers in the public schools. In many counties school funds were diverted to war purposes, but in North Carolina the state Literary Fund, which was used to supplement local funds for the support of schools, was saved from this fate by the powerful influence of Governor Vance and the State Superintendent of Schools, Calvin H. Wiley. Before the war the Southern states had depended largely on the North for textbooks, but after this source was closed, Southern presses printed texts free from Northern prejudice and filled with patriotic propaganda, such as *The First Dixie Reader,* a *Confederate Spelling Book, The Geographical Reader for Dixie Children,* and *The Southern Confederacy Arithmetic.* Crandall's *Confederate Imprints* lists nearly a hundred publications of textbooks in the Confederacy.

The demands of war disrupted the colleges and universities of the Confederate states disastrously. The draft laws did not exempt college students. The act of April 16, 1862, conscripted young men between the ages of eighteen and thirty-five, and on February 17, 1864, Congress lowered the draft age to include youths seventeen years old for state defense. Moreover, some states, such as South Carolina, drafted sixteen-year-olds for emergency military service within the state. Bell Wiley's study of a large sample of Confederate soldiers reveals, however, that only one in twenty was under eighteen years of age. Several of the University presidents, notably David L. Swain of the University of North Carolina and President Landon C. Garland of the University of Alabama, were able to secure temporary exemptions for juniors and seniors, for the reason that the Confederacy could not afford to grind up the "seed corn" of its future leadership. But in the last year of the struggle these exemptions were withdrawn, for Lee desperately needed soldiers to defend Richmond.

The force that was most powerful in closing the universities and colleges was not the draft, but the en masse volunteering of the students. The Mississippi legislature *House Journal,* November 1861, described this phenomenon as follows: "The University was not therefore suspended by any act of the Board (of Trustees) or of the Faculty, though several neighboring colleges were so, about the same time; but in the manner just described [namely, the volunteering of the students] the dissolution was spontaneous. . . ." All of the Mississippi colleges suspended operations for the duration of the war, except Mississippi College, a Baptist institution which reduced its function to that of a preparatory school. The students of South Carolina College, the university at Columbia, were not stirred to leave the college en masse until a federal fleet captured Port Royal in November 1861. The enthusiasm among the students for volunteering then became so strong that President A. B. Longstreet appealed to the governor to aid him in keeping the students in college, but having no success, he abandoned his position as president and the college closed its doors. Among the men's colleges of Georgia, only Mercer University remained open throughout the war. Wesleyan Female College, destined to be one of the oldest women's colleges in the country, also remained open and in fact grew in numbers during the course of the war, with 244 students enrolled in 1864. Many of the professors of the colleges and universities, notably the LeConte brothers, James Woodrow, Caleb Huse, A. T. Bledsoe, and John W. Mallet, rendered valuable service to the Confederate government and army.

Several of the stronger universities and medical schools managed to survive during the war period but on a very reduced basis. The University of Virginia was one of these, but its enrollment declined from six hundred students in 1861 to forty in January 1863. At the University of Alabama, which remained open until Wilson's cavalry destroyed some of its buildings near the end of the war, the students were almost entirely boys of fifteen and sixteen. The enrollment of students at the University of North Carolina was cut in the first year of the war to one-third of the normal number; in the fall of 1864, only sixty students registered for classes, and when the Union cavalry occupied Chapel Hill in April 1865, only twelve students were attending classes. As to the professors, in a faculty of fourteen members in 1860, five volunteered for service in the army, while of those who remained eight were either clergymen or too old to fight. It is ironic that the University of North Carolina was able to remain open during the conflict, but was forced to close its doors for a period of five years, from 1870 to 1875, during Reconstruction.

By far the greatest cultural loss the South sustained during the War for Southern Independence — one from which it did not recover for a whole generation — was the death of thousands of educated and promising young men in battle or from disease. They had formed the officer class, who, because they led their troops in battle, were killed in greater numbers proportionately than were the common soldiers. In addition to this decimation of the flower of aristocratic youth, another incalculable loss in culture and leadership to the post-war South resulted from the deprivation of many of the survivers of a college education that they would have obtained had not the war and the consequent impoverishment of the South occurred. Kate Stone of Brockenburn Plantation lamented in her journal that her teen-age brothers would miss obtaining a college education as a result of the long war. William Gilmore Simms expressed a similar sentiment in a letter to John Reuben Thompson, May 15, 1864, telling him that his son Gilmore would be passing through Richmond and would call on him. He observed that though his son was amiable and intelligent, three years of service in the army had "abridged his educational advantages very materially." Yet service in the Confederate army was not a total cultural loss for many of the young veterans. They had gone through an experience that deepened their knowledge of men and strengthened their characters, or as Justice Oliver Wendell Holmes, who fought on the opposite side, expressed it in a memorial address nearly twenty years after the close of the war, "through our great good fortune, in our youth our hearts were touched with fire." Like Holmes, whose Civil War diary reveals that he was often disgusted with army life and believed that the Union army could never defeat the South, the Confederate veterans as the years passed transformed the crass realities of war into something noble and glorious. For them and their descendants the lost cause passed into the realm of emotion and myth.

FIVE

The Mood of the South
after Appomattox

ON APRIL 14, 1865, THE UNITED STATES FLAG ROSE SLOWLY above the ruined Fort Sumter. General Robert Anderson, who four years before had surrendered the fort to the Confederates, was present and in a brief speech thanked God that he had lived to see this day. Henry Ward Beecher, the famous Northern preacher who had stirred up hatred against the South before the war with his violent sermons, delivered a long exultant speech on the occasion. The venerable newspaper, the *Charleston Courier,* now a Unionist newspaper, reported that about three thousand persons, including four or five hundred citizens, were in attendance. "The enthusiasm," the reporter wrote, "was unbounded. There was a simultaneous rising, cheering, waving of hats and kerchiefs for fully fifteen minutes." The same paper reported on the day before that news of the evacuation of Richmond by the Confederate government was received with rejoicing by the citizens of Charleston. "The people of the South," said the *Courier,* "are heart-

111

ily tired and disgusted with the rebellion and desire an early cessation of hostilities. Nothing can be gained by a farther [*sic*] clash at arms."

But this was not the mood of the great majority of Southern people. For them the War for Southern Independence had ended suddenly and disastrously. Whitelaw Reid, who was one of the earliest war correspondents to rush to Richmond after the surrender and who later toured the defeated Confederacy, reported that outside of Virginia few Southerners anticipated the sudden collapse of the Confederacy, though many believed that the gray-clad army was in desperate straits. Mrs. Chesnut lamented in her diary on April 7, "Richmond has fallen and I have no heart to write about it. . . . Blue black is our horizon." However, she and perhaps a majority of the Confederates were resigned, even glad, to lose their slave property. The eloquent Dr. Benjamin Palmer in a sermon in Columbia on September 21, 1864, had thanked God that slavery was doomed the world over. And the beautiful daughter of General Preston, "Buck," whom General Hood courted, exclaimed, when Mrs. Chesnut's husband portrayed a hopeless, poverty-stricken future for Southerners, "But [with] no slaves, thank God!"

A profound mood of discouragement and pessimism affected the Southerners as a whole after the conclusion of the war. This state of mind is reflected in the diary of George Anderson Mercer, a young lawyer of Savannah and a Princeton graduate, who had served as an officer in the Confederate Army (manuscript in the Southern Collection of the University of North Carolina). Although he tried to take up the broken threads of his life by returning to the practice of law, he could make very little money from his profession. He expressed the plight of thousands of the formerly privileged class of his region when he recorded in his diary, on June 18, 1865, "For the first time in my life I feel the pressure of want." He tried to exclude from his mind bitter memories and distressing reflections by absorption in reading and in his legal work, but he wrote in despair in his diary on July 9, 1865, "I have no country, no flag, no emblems, no public spirit. . . . I live now simply to live, and for my family."

For many months after the fall of the Confederacy, the Southern people tried to explain to themselves why the tragic event had occurred. Was it because the providence of God was against them and on the side of the Yankees? Benjamin Truman, the New England secretary of President Johnson, who was sent forth in the fall of 1865 to find out the temper of the people in the former Confederacy, reported to the president that he had found a deep and growing conviction among Southerners that Providence (or the Infinite) had been against the South in the recent war. Some of the ex-Confederates interpreted the inscrutable ways of Providence in permitting the Yankees to win as a judgment of God upon the Southern cause because of the speculation and war profiteering (which actually seems to have been much less than in the North) and because of His anger at the Southern people for their failure to be sufficiently religious.

Strangely, to modern eyes, they seldom attributed the defeat of their cause to the sin of slavery, for as a whole they did not believe the ownership of slaves to be a sin. John William De Forest, the Freedmen's Bureau officer stationed in Greenville, South Carolina, in 1867, noted that the Southerners in the Greenville District with whom he talked would not admit that slavery was the cause of the war. Most Southerners maintained that the war was not fought over the issue of the preservation of slavery but over states rights or constitutional liberty. George Anderson Mercer of Savannah wrote in his diary, July 9, 1865, "I have survived a cause as just as was ever espoused," and Gayarré wrote on May 31 to his Northern friend Evert Duyckinck, "we, still think we were supporting the holiest of causes," but the South would submit to "Heaven's verdict." Nevertheless, one of the most striking aspects of the Southern mood after Appomattox was the wide-spread expression of approval, even relief, that slavery had been abolished. Ex-Governor Henry A. Wise of Virginia, for example, declared in an address on June 17, 1873, before Roanoke College that slavery was the worst curse that had ever rested on the Southern people and that it had been a great incubus on Southern development.

Almost universally the Southern people maintained that the Confederacy had been overcome because the North had unfairly called in mercenary European immigrants to fill the ranks of their armies. There was some truth in this contention, for Miss Ella Lonn in her study, *Foreigners in the Confederacy,* found that foreign-born soldiers constituted from one-fifth to one-fourth of the strength of the Union army. John T. Trowbridge, a Northern journalist who toured the battlefields in the summer and winter of 1865, talked with an ex-Confederate soldier at Manassas, who expressed a typical sentiment when he emphatically declared that the Confederate Army was never whipped, but the North had overpowered the South by getting foreigners and "the niggers" to help them. Whitelaw Reid was told that the Southerners were the bravest people on earth; yet a Georgia planter in discussing the subject with the Northern journalist had some reservations about the calibre of the Western troops, whom he did not think were up to the standard of courage and fighting ability of the eastern army under Lee — an army, he declared, that was composed of gentlemen.

Southerners bitterly resented the use by the North of Negro troops, many of whom were slaves recruited from Kentucky and the occupied regions of the South. There was something ignoble they thought in the eagerness of Northern states to recruit Negroes from the South, even using brokers, to fill out their quotas in the draft and thus avoid conscripting some of their white men. Two hundred thousand Negro soldiers served during the course of the war in the Union

army. This is a significant number when it is correlated with
the fact that the Confederate Army at the peak of its strength,
which was reached in June 1863 just before the battle of
Gettysburg, had only 261,000 men reported as present for
duty. During the Reconstruction period the Negroes cited
as one reason justifying their demand for political and civil
rights the fact that Negro troops had fought bravely in the
battles of Olustee, Milligan's Bend, Petersburg, and the storm-
ing of Fort Wagner at Charleston.

In assessing the causes for their defeat Southerners were too
proud to admit that after Gettysburg the Confederate people
had lost the will to fight. This defeatism was indicated by the
tremendous amount of desertion. The Richmond *Dispatch*
observed, "On many a hard fought field the tide of success
would have turned overwhelmingly in our favor had all been
present whom duty required to participate in the strife."
J. D. B. De Bow wrote to his friend Charles Gayarré on
February 3, 1865, that the Confederacy was crowded with
"whipped men and reconstructionists." The New Orleans editor bluntly observed that there was not much "heroic stuff"
left in the country — the only hope of salvation was foreign
aid. It was consoling, however, to the ego of Southern people
to blame someone else than themselves for the failure of their
effort to establish a Southern republic. Eliza Andrews, the
daughter of Judge Garnett Andrews of Georgia, wrote in her
journal on April 21, 1865, after General Robert Toombs had
confirmed the rumor of Lee's surrender on April 9th: "Europe
has quietly folded her hands and beheld a noble nation perish."

The most extreme element of unreconciled Confederates
left the country after the war. Some of these who had been
prominent in urging secession fled to Europe or Canada.
Among the latter was Robert Toombs, who later returned
but remained hostile to the North and unreconstructed to
the day of his death in 1885. There was also an emigration of
Southerners, especially soldiers and officers, to Mexico and to

Brazil where slavery still existed. The Mexican emperor, Maximilian, offered generous terms to Southern immigrants and appointed Matthew F. Maury, famous oceanographer and Confederate commodore, as commissioner of immigration. Some prominent Confederate leaders such as Generals Sterling Price, Jo Shelby, and Kirby Smith, and Governors Isham Harris of Tennessee and Henry W. Allen of Louisiana joined the movement to Mexico, which resulted in the founding of the colony of Carlotta, seventy miles west of Veracruz, and the immigration of approximately 2,300 former Confederates. The movement of ex-Confederates to Brazil was considerably larger. Led by the rector of St. Philips Church in New Orleans, Ballard S. Dunn, and the filibusterer, Lunsford Warren Hastings, between four and six thousand ex-Confederates founded settlements in Brazil, one named "Little America." But Robert E. Lee, Wade Hampton, L. Q. C. Lamar, and John B. Gordon discouraged Southerners from leaving the defeated South and urged them to stay and help rebuild its shattered civilization. Probably a much larger number of ex-Confederates were held back from emigrating to Latin-America by their extreme poverty.

Instead of seeking to emigrate, many soldiers in the defeated Confederate Army had a great longing to return to their homes and forget this tragic episode in their lives. One of the latter was a Major in Wade Hampton's cavalry, Minor Jackson Hough, who after the surrender rode back to his home in the up-country village of Chesterfield, South Carolina. As he was passing by one of the Virginia battlefields, according to the tradition of his family, a sudden mood of disgust for the war and for the loss of four years of his life overcame him, and, impulsively drawing his sword, he flung it upon the battlefield in a symbolic act of dismissing the unhappy past from his memory. Never afterwards was he willing to talk about the war; he wished only to look to the future.

As the war-worn veterans returned to their homes many

of them had not a cent of valid money and were disreputable in appearance. Eliza Andrews wrote in her journal of those who at the end of the war passed through the little village of Washington, Georgia. "Some of our friends pass on without stopping to see us because they say they are too ragged and dirty to show themselves — the son of the richest man in New Orleans trudged through the other day, with no coat on his back, no shoes on his feet." She noted that the defeated soldiers in gray did not "whine over their altered fortunes and ruined prospects," but they were filled with pathos in contemplating the fate of their ruined country.

The bitterest feeling toward the Yankees was not displayed by the soldiers and officers, but by the women. Eliza Andrews and her friends, for example, whenever they met Northern soldiers on the streets would not look at them. Her aunt would not invite the Yankee soldier who guarded their house to eat with the family, with the result that he resentfully left his post. Eliza had so little money immediately after the war that she could not send a letter; she thought of rolling cigarettes and selling them to soldiers to get pocket money, but then she commented, "only I could not bear the humiliation." Southern women often went to great lengths not to walk in the street where the United States flag floated from houses and buildings. Wherever Trowbridge went on his tour of the South immediately after the war, he found that the men felt thoroughly "whipped" and quiet but the women were extremely resentful and vindictive; the daughter of his landlady in Charlestown, Virginia, he described as "a Southern fire [eater] incarnate," vigorously outspoken in expressing her scorn of Yankees.

When Ellie Swain, the beautiful and vivacious daughter of the president of the University of North Carolina on August 23, 1865, married General Smith Atkins of Illinois, who had commanded the Union Cavalry that occupied Chapel Hill at the close of the war, many of the citizens showed their bitter mood. Very few attended the wedding and some of those invited spat on the wedding invitations. Also, President Swain, who accepted a fine horse as a gift from the Yankee general during the course of the brief courtship, lost the confidence and support of the state. Cornelia Phillips Spencer, one of the friends of the Swain family and the great feminine intellectual of the village, forgave the family for the marriage, but for years she disliked the "Yankee nation." Although she agreed intellectually with the policy of reconciliation as the best course for the South, she wrote in August 1865, "as for my own single self I desire to have as little as possible to do with the Northern people . . . I do not love my country. I feel rather as if I had no country. . . ." Nevertheless, at the end of 1865 in her diary she predicted that, though the South would have a hard road to travel in recovering from the effects of the war, within ten years it would be infinitely better off than it had ever been. Reading her diary in 1900, she noted, "It took thirty years."

Most Southern people were especially resentful of the Yankee "nigger teachers" who invaded their communities to uplift the freedmen. They completely ostracized them, not condescending even to speak to them. One of the Northern schoolteachers, Cornelia Hancock, wrote in a letter from Mount Pleasant, near Charleston, South Carolina, "Every one hates us with a bitter hatred here." One reason for such hostility observed Edward King, who toured the South in 1873 for *Scribner's Magazine* and published a book about his experiences entitled *The Great South,* was a belief among Southerners that the Northern school teachers put false ideas into the heads of the Negroes, particularly of the women.

The presence of Negro troops and garrisons in the Southern states was also very odious to the people. It was regarded as an unnecessary humiliation of the proud Southerners, just as the defeated Germans after World War I resented the use of Negro soldiers by the French as occupation troops in the

Rhine Valley. Negro officers took delight in executing the order against the wearing of rebel uniforms by stopping former Confederate soldiers who were too poor to buy civilian clothes and cutting off the buttons bearing the insignia, "C. S. A." Congressman Harvey M. Watterson, the father of "Marse Henry," the famous editor of the Louisville *Courier-Journal,* wrote President Johnson from Newbern, North Carolina, on June 20, 1865, that at least 3,000 Negro troops were stationed in the town and that the citizens felt that they did not deserve such punishment. He recommended that both these troops and the brigade of Negro troops in Raleigh should be removed. In South Carolina the *Charleston Courier* reported on June 13, 1865, that the planters feared that the colored troops sent into the interior would demoralize the Negro laborers.

Another source of keeping alive hatred of the victorious North was the humiliating treatment of Jefferson Davis while he was a war prisoner in Fort Monroe. A chain and iron ball was put on his leg, a humiliation that he resisted with a physical struggle. To protest this degradation of the ex-President of the Confederacy the women of Richmond wore mourning veils, and though at the end of the war he had been unpopular, he became revered as a martyr.

But the resentment of Sherman's outrages on the civilian population in his march through Georgia and South Carolina lived much longer in Southern memories. John R. Dennett, a Harvard graduate who traveled through the South in 1865 and wrote articles for *The Nation,* found the hatred for the North more intense in Columbia, South Carolina, than in any other city he visited. The driver of the stage coach in which Dennett was riding could hardly contain his anger as he described the marauding of Sherman's soldiers, who took everything in his humble house, "even down to my little girl's doll-clothes." Other passengers vowed personal vengeance on Sherman. An intelligent Negro barber of Newbern, North

Carolina, told Dennett that the conduct of Sherman's bummers, who ransacked nearly every Negro house in the town, had alienated the Negroes from this type of Northerner.

The South that emerged after the surrender at Appomattox was racked by the violent hatreds that had survived between secessionists, "the secesh," and the Unionists. John R. Dennett met a Confederate sympathizer in Virginia who had fled from East Tennessee, a Unionist stronghold, because he had felt that his life was in danger if he remained. Whitelaw Reid talked to an Alabamian who protested against the iron-clad oath required of Southerners appointed to local office, saying that the federal government would be able to get only "wimmen" and "niggahs" to fill the office of postmaster, and that "if you fetch any d - d tories [Unionists] heah, that went agin their State, and so kin take the oath, I tell ye, twill soon be too hot to hold them! We haint got no use for sich."

Trowbridge described "an unrelenting spirit of persecution shown toward Union men in Mississippi." He also recorded that Tennessee Governor Brownlow was both an ardent Unionist and a Negro-hater, and observed that it was hard to tell which group the people of East Tennessee hated most, former rebels or Negroes. With the strong support of the members from the eastern part of the state, the Tennessee legislature had just defeated a Negro Testimony bill. In a region west of Chapel Hill, North Carolina, Dennett (riding horseback through the country), was told that the Unionists continued to attack and rob the houses of secessionists — that those who had hid in the woods to avoid the conscript officers had learned to become bushwhackers — a practice that they continued after the war. In areas of strong Unionist sentiment assaults were made on leading Confederates, who accordingly found it prudent to absent themselves from election gatherings and other public assemblages. Furthermore, bushwhackers and demobilized soldiers without means of support engaged in robberies, murders, and the terrorization of some communi-

ties. In Texas, Edward King reported that during the first
two years following the war a thousand murders a year occurred. Much of this lawlessness resulted from the habit of
carrying concealed weapons and the widespread consumption
of alcoholic beverages.

Moreover, the extreme poverty of the Southern people after
the surrender at Appomattox produced profound discouragement throughout the land. Kenneth Rayner, a leading North
Carolina Unionist, wrote to President Johnson on July 8,
1865, "Your Excellency can have no conception of the utter
and absolute poverty of the people of the Southern states.
There is no money here, literally none." The farmers had
virtually no staple crops — cotton, tobacco, naval stores —
to sell for cash, and there were no banks to lend money. A
symbol of Southern poverty was the lack of decent clothes
for the people to wear. When the Northern schoolteacher,
Cornelia Hancock, went through Virginia and North Carolina on her way to South Carolina, she was shocked by the
desolate and poverty-stricken appearance of the land and the
people, commenting that the sparseness of their clothes made
the inhabitants look so badly. Two years after the close of the
war De Forest noted that "at least half of the villagers of
upper South Carolina and nearly all the country people wore
gray or butternut homespun; even Governor Perry, the great
man of the place, had his homespun suit and occasionally
attended court in it."

The Northern journalists who traveled in the South found
social and economic conditions extremely depressing and
desolate. They saw very little of the legendary grandeur of
the Old South that the abolitionists and the novelists had
depicted. Rather they observed that most of the people lived
in log cabins or unpretentious frame houses. Trowbridge noted
the monotony of seeing crude log cabins, with no glass windows and their doors kept open; the hotels were miserable,
and the roads primitive. The language of the people was

illiterate and archaic; for instance, the verb "helped" was usually "holped," "where" was "whar," "there," "thar," "get," "git." The typical Southern meal, Dennett wrote, was cornbread, bacon, greens or black-eyed peas, buttermilk, or execrable coffee, often without sugar or milk — essentially the diet of the slaves in the pre-war South. Sidney Andrews, who traveled through the South in 1865 as correspondent of the Boston *Advertiser,* thought that the Southerners, in contrast to the Yankees, were stupidly opposed to ordinary physical comforts (a survival of frontier attitudes), and that their methods of cooking food ruined its taste.

Especially were Northerners impressed with the idleness, apathy, and laziness of most of the Southerners whom they observed. The energetic Cornelia Hancock was disgusted at seeing so many Southern women of the lower class sitting on the porch with hands on their laps simply doing nothing. She noted that the people were too lazy even to remove logs that had fallen on the road; instead they went around them. When a train arrived at the lonely little villages, half of the male population was at the station out of curiosity. Some travelers observed that only the Negroes were working, an ironic commentary on the constant iterations of Southerners that the Negro would not work in freedom. Trowbridge thought that the planters lacked energy and ambition — were a helpless set of people. Much of the indolence of the people (aside from the enervating influence of the climate and diseases such as malaria and hookworm), was attributed to the fact that business was at a standstill except in a few favored towns such as Atlanta, Mobile, and New Orleans. Because there was a great scarcity of money, people resorted to barter, and often merchants could not sell goods because they could not give change. Farmers were tremendously handicapped by the scarcity of work animals, for the depredations of both armies had taken most of the horses and mules. Furthermore, large numbers of idle, apathetic whites seemed to have been stunned by the collapse of the old order, and though penniless, were too proud to work as day laborers as the Negroes did.

The deep mood of discouragement in many parts of the South lingered at least until home rule was established and the carpetbaggers had retired. In 1868 Jabez L. M. Curry, who was destined to become the greatest educational reformer of his section, was so pessimistic about the outlook in the lower South that he decided to give up his post as president of Howard College at Marion, Alabama, and move to Richmond. He explained his decision as follows: "It seemed unwise to keep my wife and children under radical misrule, and to remain where a generation or more would be needed to recover from the disastrous consequences of the War and hostile legislation." Colonel Richard M. Johnston, also, as the result of the war and the emancipation of his slaves had lost (he estimated in his autobiography) $50,000, a small fortune at that time. He was so discouraged over the outlook of living in postwar Georgia that he sold his plantation and moved to Baltimore. Here he established his Pen Lucy School for boys, which was largely patronized by Southern youth. When he became a Roman Catholic in 1875 it declined so in enrollment that he abandoned it eight years later and supported himself until his death in 1898 by his writings and a small federal job in Washington.

During this dark period Sidney Lanier was struggling to make a precarious living with temporary jobs as a hotel clerk in Montgomery, then as a teacher in an academy at Prattville, Alabama, later as a lawyer in Macon, and finally as a musician and lecturer in Baltimore. While he was a hotel clerk in Montgomery, he wrote to his Northern friend Milton Northrup, June 29, 1866, of the benumbing effect of the war upon the economic life of the town: "I despair of giving you any idea of the mortal stagnation which paralyzes all business here. On our streets Monday is very like Sunday: they show no life, save late in the afternoon, when the girls come out, one

by one, and shine and move just as the stars do an hour later."
Sharing the feeling of his section about the oppression of the
South by the reconstruction measures, he expressed it in his
poems, "Laughter in the Senate," "The Raven Days," and
particularly, "Civil Rights," written in the dialect of a Georgia
cracker. This poem protested against the adoption of the Civil
Rights Bill, introduced in 1874 in Congress, which gave Negroes equality of rights in trains, hotels, theaters, and in jury
service. The old farmer in the poem who had lost a son in
the Confederate Army says:

> But now, as I was sayin' when I jest had come to see
> My way was clear to like 'em [the Northerners] and to
>   treat 'em brotherlee;
> When every nigger's son is schooled (I payin' of the tax,
> For not a mother's son of 'em has more than's on ther
>   backs),
> And when they crowds and stinks me off from gittin' to
>   the polls
> While Congress grinds ther grain, as 'twere, 'thout takin
>   of no tolls;
> And when I stand aside and waits, and hopes that things
>   will mend,
> Here comes this Civil Rights and says, this fuss shan't
>   have no end!

Accordingly, he continued to feel deeply discouraged over
the prospects of the South. To his brother Clifford in Georgia,
he wrote on June 8, 1879, urging him to join him in Baltimore, "I cannot contemplate with any patience your stay in
the South. In my soberest moments I can perceive no outlook
for that land. . . . And thus, as I said, it really seems as if any
prosperity at the South must come long after your time and
mine. . . . Whatever is to be done, you and I can do our part
of it far better here than there. Come away." He commented
that he thought the South was poorer then than it had been at
the end of the war. Also at this time Lanier was depressed over
political prospects, for he thought that the South was miser-
ably represented in Congress. During the following year, he

published an essay in *Century Magazine* on "The New South" in which he declared that the salvation of the South rested on the growth of small farms and a diversified industry. Still the South remained for many years a bleak section of the nation for anyone with the intellectual and artistic interests of the Lanier brothers.

After the emancipation of the slaves a deep mood of pessimism in regard to the future of agriculture in the South had darkened the minds especially of the older planters. Much of their discouragement arose from their profound skepticism about the reliability of Negro labor without the discipline of slavery. Whitelaw Reid wrote from Alabama in 1865 that "the old planters seemed utterly despondent about raising cotton by free negro labor. . . ." Trowbridge found a difference of opinion on the subject between the old generation of planters and the young planters, the latter having a more hopeful attitude toward the successful employment of free Negro workers. Yet it was a young planter of Alabama who declared in a conversation with Reid, "the nigger never works except when he is compelled to. . . . He'll work a day for you for good wages and then go off and spend it; and you'll not get another lick out of him till he's hungry and getting nothing to eat."

Charles Gayarré in a conversation with Edward King of *Scribner's Magazine* in 1873 also gave a gloomy account of the conduct of the freedmen. They flocked to the towns and cities; when they were employed on the plantations, they did about a third of the work accomplished by a white man in a day. Though by nature kindly, generous, and courteous, the Negro, he thought, was an inferior being, devoid of moral consciousness, ignorant, and peculiarly unfitted by slavery for the responsibilities of freedom. He anticipated that the race would disappear in Louisiana within fifty years because of want and the neglect of their health. In Georgia, Alexander H. Stephens made a similar gloomy prediction.

The most striking change in the attitude of Southerners toward Negroes in the post-war years was the abandonment of the feeling of paternalism toward them that many of the planters had shown before the war. The many conversations that John Richard Dennett held in 1865 with Southern whites, particularly of the yeoman and poor white class, revealed a strong dislike for Negroes and a desire to remove them from the country or colonize them, despite their realization that their labor was sorely needed to carry on Southern farming. They thought that the Negro in freedom would be constantly stealing — even some Negroes declared that it was useless for them to raise chickens or vegetables, or watermelons, for other Negroes would steal them. Southerners in general were vehemently opposed to giving the Negro the legal right to testify against whites in court, maintaining that he had no conception of an oath, or as a poor white in North Carolina expressed it, "a nigger's oath is not worth a chew of tobacco."

Many of the complaints of whites against the Negro laborers arose from the fact that a considerable number of employers would not pay fair wages. Some planters in the upper South would pay only five or six dollars a month to Negro workers, in addition to furnishing them and their families with a cabin and food. In the lower South, especially after economic recovery began in 1866 and a competition for labor developed, they were paid better, usually $10 a month with maintenance. Unscrupulous planters would drive Negroes off the plantation after the crops had been harvested, paying them nothing for their labor. The Freedmen's Bureau was undoubtedly a necessary institution to secure justice for the freedmen, especially in supervising labor contracts between employers and Negroes.

The attitude of many whites in regarding the freedmen as if they were still slaves did not disappear quickly after the war. The Freedmen's Bureau officers received numerous complaints from freedmen, especially from those in the interior, that they were whipped and mistreated by the old slave masters. Dennett's conversations with Negroes and with Freedmen's Bureau agents present a stark picture of human greed and cruelty in the treatment of the relatively defenseless Negro. A former slave from the deep South, to which he had been transported and sold before the war, while traveling to North Carolina to locate his relatives, told the New Englander that virtual slavery continued to survive in South Carolina. He said "a many doesn't dar to own they is got their liberty." In Atlanta, Georgia, the Freedmen's Bureau agents told Dennett that a majority of the planters were unwilling to pay adequate wages to the freedmen or recognize in practice that the Negroes were free.

Trowbridge and De Forest attributed much of the friction between planters and Negroes to the fact that both were tyros in the mystery of free labor. It took several years of experimentation, for example, to find the most satisfactory method of compensating the freedmen for their labor, resulting ultimately in the adoption of the share crop system, whereby the Negro tenant received from one-third to one-half of the crop if he furnished only his labor. Because the planters lacked money with which to pay wages, the wage system soon disappeared in the cotton country. A shortage of plantation labor in the lower South in 1866 led planters to go into neighboring states to secure field hands, a practice that increased the bargaining position of the freedmen. In the spring of 1866 John G. Troutman of Kentucky tried to operate a cotton plantation on Sicily Island in the Mississippi River. He paid commissions in New Orleans to obtain Negro laborers, but he lost this money because the Negroes soon ran away. He could not adjust his thinking and the attitudes developed in slavery days to the new situation. When he tried to whip a ten-year-old boy, he wrote to his wife in Kentucky (manuscript in the University of Kentucky Library) that two of his Negro ploughmen quit his service. Profoundly discouraged over operating a plantation with free Negro labor, he described the attitude of the Negroes as "very touchy," and the whites and blacks in his neighborhood were mutually distrustful and denunciatory. He believed that it was necessary for the state to compel workers to live up to their contracts.

In order to control the Negroes and define their rights, a special set of laws known as the Black Codes were enacted by various Southern states. These laws were derived from the apprenticeship and vagrancy laws applying to whites in the North as well as in the South, the customs of slavery times, the ante-bellum laws relating to free Negroes, British West Indies legislation for ex-slaves, and regulations of the Union Army and the Freedmen's Bureau. Passed in 1865 these laws varied in severity, the most drastic being in the regions of the largest proportion of Negroes, notably Mississippi and Louisiana. Their main purpose seems to have been to keep the Negro at work. The Mississippi law, for example, permitted not only a civil officer but any person to arrest a deserter from his employment and take him back to the plantation, where he should be required to fulfill his contract, unless there was just cause for his quitting work. It also placed heavy penalties on any one persuading or enticing a laborer from his employer or knowingly employing a deserter. The Louisiana Black Code provided that the laborer should work in summer ten hours, in winter, nine, and decreed punishment for feigning sickness, failing to obey reasonable orders, leaving the plantation without permission, impudence, swearing, or indecent language in the presence of the employer, his family, or agent. The Black Codes prohibited intermarriage between whites and blacks, forbade the sale of liquor to freedmen, and the ownership or carrying of fire-arms or bowie knives by Negroes. Vagrants were ordered arrested and fined, and if the convicted vagrant could not pay the fine levied on him, or if the freedmen should be delinquent in paying taxes, he should be hired for the shortest time to any one paying his fine or taxes, "giving preference to his employer if there be one."

The Black Codes expressed accurately the mood and opin-

ion of the Southerners as they faced the colossal problem of
establishing a stable social order and of adjusting the former
slave to the conditions of a free society. Many Northerners,
especially radical politicians, saw in these codes an attempt to
continue the practice of virtual enslavement of the Negro.
From the standpoint of conciliation of Northern public opinion alone they were a grave political mistake. Nevertheless,
they were soon rendered inoperative by the Freedmen's Bureau
and U. S. military authorities, and were repealed in 1867 when
the military governments were established.

What of the mood of the Southern Negro himself, who was
the great question mark in the mind of his former master
after his liberation. His mood has to be determined largely by
his actions. When the day of freedom came he was woefully
unprepared for his new condition. It was natural that the
Negroes' first desire was to test the reality of their freedom by
leaving the plantation, and consequently a great internal migration set in, some seeking to unite families broken up by the
slave trade, others forced off the land by former masters, but
the great majority impelled by an irresistable desire to flock to
the cities and towns. Whitelaw Reid in his *After the War; a
Tour of the Southern States in 1865-1866* described a remarkable city of log cabins and shanties built by the freedmen outside of Newbern, North Carolina, which he estimated to contain 10,000 Negroes. Near Hilton Head, South Carolina, a
Negro settlement, called Mitchellville, had its own Negro government. The migration of the Negroes, Sir George Campbell
later noted, was confined mostly to within the Southern states
and after Appomattox more Negroes came southward from
the North than went to the Northern states. Washington, D. C.,
however, received many Negro *emigrés,* estimated to number
20,000. Other ways the freedman used to test or exhibit his
freedom were to change his name and get rid of his old wife.
The Negro women, in turn, in imitation of the white ladies,
often refused to work in the fields.

The great amount of idleness that developed among the

Negroes after they were liberated was due partly to their unwillingness to sign labor contracts because they believed that they would be given "forty acres and a mule" by the federal government. The Port Royal, South Carolina, experiment had done much to foster this idea. The Union Navy occupied the harbor of Port Royal, and nearby Hilton Head and Beaufort in 1862. The sea coast planters abandoned their homes and the Negroes were left in possession. The plantations of the refugee planters were confiscated, and their lands were divided into small farms and given to the former slaves. General Rufus Saxton, an ardent Negrophile, was placed in charge of the freedmen on the sea islands (really not islands in the ocean but the littoral, divided by small rivers), and he settled thirty thousand Negroes on them. These Negroes were coal black in color and among the most ignorant of their race in the South, yet they made remarkable progress aided by the advice of Northern superintendents and teachers. General Saxton told Whitelaw Reid in the fall of 1865 that these Negroes (about 17,000 of them remaining) had become self-sustaining and that the rations furnished by the government had been in large part paid back by them. The Reverend Richard Fuller, a Baptist preacher who had been one of the dispossessed planters and had settled in Baltimore, returned with Reid's party to his old plantation on St. Helena Island and reported that the Negroes had performed well in cultivating the land. But after Johnson's May 1865 proclamation of pardon and restoration of plantations, many of these Negroes lost the lands they had cultivated, General Saxton was superseded, and the new commandant was favorable to the planters rather than to the Negroes. A Negro settlement at Davis Bend, below Vicksburg, on the plantations of Jefferson and Joseph Davis met a similar fate. At the close of 1865 Trowbridge had visited the settlement and found about three hundred Negroes settled at Davis Bend, living on about five thousand acres divided into small farms. The Negroes paid a rent to the government and produced 2,500 bales of cotton, thus earning money to buy mules and plows. The experiment was proving "a signal success"; the colony was self-governing and imposed severe sentences in court on trifling and lazy Negroes, who injured the reputation of the settlement, but the colony was dispersed when the land was returned to its former owners.

Most Southerners of this period believed that the Negro's failings were due to inherited characteristics, but it is now obvious that they were in large part the result of the institution of slavery. Stanley Elkins in a modern study of Southern slavery has compared "the peculiar institution" in conditioning the Negro slaves to the German concentration camps in World War II. Just as the white prisoners of those camps were conditioned to habits of obedience, dependence, loss of a sense of responsibility, in fact, a child-like behavior, the slaves developed similar characteristics or intensified habits that their ancestors had brought from Africa. Travelers in the South after the war noted that the Negroes of the up-country who had been associated with small white farmers as well as the Negroes of the towns and cities were much more intelligent than the Gullah Negroes of lowland South Carolina and Georgia who lived on lonely large plantations having little contact with white people. Sidney Andrews wrote that the city and country Negroes were as much unlike as two different races — the country Negro was in character what slavery had made of him, idle, improvident, negligent, immoral, and prone to stealing. Though this observation was undoubtedly an exaggeration, it contained considerable truth.

Two very favorable aspects of the mood or thought of the Negroes in the trying period of readjustment after the war were his poignant desire to learn to read and write and the absence of a vindictive spirit toward his former masters or the Southern whites. The great enthusiasm for schools shown by the freedmen, and his strong desire to own land were noted by the Northern travelers and schoolteachers who came South after the war. The Negroes at this time manifested a greater desire for education than the poor whites. Moreover, the Negroes in general accepted without any great protest the segregation of schools. While the carpetbaggers demanded the disfranchisement of the Southern whites who aided the rebellion, some of the most prominent Negro leaders, such as Senators Hiram Revels and Blanche Bruce, favored lenient treatment of the Southern whites. Gayarré wrote on March 28, 1867, to Bancroft, who he thought had become bitterly prejudiced against the South, that even the Negro newspaper, the *New Orleans Tribune,* was opposed to the disfranchisement of the whites and in favor of majority rule and a republican government for the state.

The mood of a people finds its ultimate expression in politics. The Southern people looked anxiously toward Washington to see what policy President Johnson and Congress would adopt in regard to reconstruction. Whitelaw Reid, a precocious young man of radical sympathies, in 1865 reported that for several months after the surrender at Appomattox, the Southern people were so dispirited and cowed that they would have accepted virtually any terms, including Negro suffrage, that the federal government might impose. In his book about the South he described a discussion that he heard in a tavern in Meridian, Mississippi, in November 1865, in which one of the group declared, "Last spring, you can form no conception of the utter, abject humiliation of the Southern people. We were all prostrate, helpless, abased to the dust, but out of this abject condition Mr. Johnson has partly lifted us. He has made us feel that we have some standing ground, some chance still to battle for our rights. . . ."

His reference was to President Johnson's proclamation of May 29 which restored civil government to North Carolina and outlined a generous policy of amnesty. The proclamation granted pardons to those swearing allegiance to the United

States, excepting the high Confederate civil and military officers and those owning more than $20,000 worth of taxable property. Individuals of these excluded classes could apply to the president for special pardons, and Johnson issued 13,500 of these pardons, of which one-half were granted to that class of men whom he had so violently denounced, the owners of more than $20,000 worth of property. One of the most important consequences of this liberal amnesty policy was that it restored many of the confiscated plantations that the radicals and Negroes had hoped would be retained to give small farms to the freedmen.

The president sent some prominent men, both Northerners and Southerners, into the South in 1865 as observers to report on the mood of the people. One of these was General Grant, who on December 18 reported that the mass of thinking men in the defeated Confederacy accepted the decisions of the war in abolishing slavery and establishing the supremacy of the federal government and that they would cooperate in good faith with the federal government in the adoption of any plan of restoring civil government that would not be humiliating to them as citizens. Even more encouraging were the letters that Harvey M. Watterson, a Unionist Congressman from Tennessee, sent to Johnson in June and July from North Carolina. Here, and in Virginia, he wrote, the citizens were badly whipped men, who declared that they had had enough of war to last them the remainder of their days. He was convinced that the future loyalty of the state of North Carolina was certain. The people were now praising the president for his generous amnesty policy, his suspension of the collection of the iniquitous cotton tax which would save fifty million dollars to Southerners, and he observed, "Your position on Negro suffrage is doing more than anything else to win the confidence of the people of North Carolina." Benjamin Truman also declared in his report to the president that the returned soldiers and officers of the Confederate army were "infinitely more wearied and disgusted with war and all its works than those of our army and long for nothing so much as quiet." The veterans, he thought, representing "the backbone and sinew of the South," were the most potent force in promoting reconciliation with the North and a speedy reconstruction of the Union.

There were, however, dissenting voices to this favorable report on the Southern mood, chiefly from men of radical views. Carl Schurz, who spent three months in the summer of 1865 touring the South, was one of the hostile critics. The people were not impressed, he wrote, with the criminality of their rebellion against the national government, and there was still an utter absence of national feeling among the Southern people. He believed that if they had the opportunity they would attempt to establish in place of outright slavery some species of compulsory labor, such as serfdom or peonage. The Negro, therefore, should be granted the franchise as a protection of his rights, and the acceptance of Negro suffrage should be made a condition of the admission of the former Confederate States into the Union. Sharing the views of Schurz concerning the South's intransigence were Trowbridge and Dennett, who thought that the South was biding its time, waiting for the removal of federal troops in order to resume its old ways.

After Johnson manifested a policy of reconciliation and leniency to the defeated section, a resurgence of hope arose in the South. The new feeling was evident in the fall elections of 1865. The Southerners believed that the rebellion had not changed their fundamental rights under the Constitution and that they were entitled to the same constitutional rights that citizens of the North enjoyed. In order to restore the seceded states to their normal relation with the federal government, Johnson had followed Lincoln's policy of appointing or recognizing provisional governors, men who had been Unionists in 1860-61 — Michael Hahn in Louisiana, "Parson" William G.

Brownlow in Tennessee, and Francis Pierrepont in Virginia. Johnson himself appointed provisional governors in seven of the former Confederate states — men who were much like himself, Unionists, believers in state's rights, with a Southern attitude toward the Negro. The most prominent of these leaders were Benjamin F. Perry in South Carolina, William W. Holden, influential Raleigh editor and leader during the Civil War of the peace movement in North Carolina, and Andrew Jackson Hamilton in Texas.

Under the direction of these officials elections were held for delegates to state constitutional conventions. Only white men who had taken the oath of allegiance and had been pardoned were permitted to vote in the elections. The conventions that assembled in the fall of 1865, as well as the governments formed under the plan of presidential reconstruction, were dominated by the old Whig element of the voters, for the radical secessionists had been discredited by the defeat of their cause. Sidney Andrews, the Boston correspondent, gave careful reports of the North Carolina, South Carolina, and Georgia conventions that he attended. All the Southern conventions repealed the secession ordinances, abolished slavery, and all but South Carolina repudiated the state debts incurred in aiding the Confederate government. None of the conventions adopted Negro suffrage or provisions for allowing them to sit on juries or testify in court against whites in cases in which they were not involved.

President Johnson believed that in the new governments set up after the war the yeomen would reject as candidates for office the old aristocratic leaders who had led them astray and would elect men from their own ranks. But they disappointed him by choosing as their political representatives the old leaders whom they respected, including the election to the Senate by Georgia of the former vice president of the Confederacy. In the elections of November 1865, the people elected to Congress war heroes and men who after secession had gone with their state. Some of the candidates appealed directly to the voters to elect them to office on their Confederate record. Certain astute Southerners, such as Wade Hampton in South Carolina, realized that it would be highly impolitic for prominent leaders in the Confederacy to seek state or federal office. Therefore he refused to become a candidate, though he could have easily been elected governor over the successful candidate, James Orr. The loyalty of the Southern people to the leaders who fought in the War for Southern Independence was the main reason why every one of the Southern states, except Tennessee, in 1866 rejected the Fourteenth Amendment, which prohibited the former Confederate leaders from holding office in either state or national government.

The mood of the South in the years 1865-67 explains to a large degree some of the serious mistakes that the Southern people made at this time — mistakes that aided Northern radicals in imposing a harsh reconstruction upon the section. The Southerners were short-sighted in enacting some of the laws for the regulation of the Negroes, the so-called Black Codes, and in failing to give to those Negroes who were qualified by education and ownership of property the right to vote. President Johnson suggested that they do so (though he did not insist upon it) as a matter of policy to placate Northern public opinion, or as he put it, "to disarm the adversary" — the radicals in Congress. The Southern people were certainly wrong in ostracizing the "Northern school marms" who came South to teach and elevate the freedmen. They made a grave tactical error also in 1865 in electing to Congress prominent Confederate officials and generals. It was unfortunate for the South, too, that at this critical time serious race riots occurred in New Orleans and Memphis in which many Negroes were killed. The mistakes that the Southerners made were compounded by the folly of President Johnson in Washington and in his "swing-around-the-circle" speeches before the crucial Congressional elections in the fall of 1866. Finally, the rejec-

tion of the Fourteenth Amendment in that year by the Southern states was a serious blunder, bringing upon their land a
drastic reconstruction, with military government, that they
probably could have avoided by accepting the amendment.
Thus the following decade of political turmoil, which gave rise
to "the black legend of Reconstruction" (though true in part),
delayed the reconciliation of the South and North for another
generation. The accomplishment of that reconciliation was
noted by Lord Bryce in his classic *American Commonwealth,*
when he wrote in 1888, "Hostility to the Northern people has
almost disappeared." Ten years later the reconciliation of the
two sections was demonstrated to the world in the Spanish-
American War.

SIX

The Waning of the Old South
Civilization

SOUTHERNERS OF THE POST-CIVIL WAR GENERATION TENDED
to date events by whether they happened before or after the
Civil War. The Civil War was their most vivid experience,
one that lasted long in their memories. It appeared to them
so tragic and cataclysmic that it marked the end of an era
which they glamorized, and the beginning of another era less
romantic, comfortable, and serene than "the days before the
war." To the cultural and social historian, however, there was
a continuity between the pre-Civil War civilization and the
society that has been designated as the "New South." In a
real sense, despite an outward facade of revolutionary change,
the civilization of the Old South continued long after its
epitaph had been announced by Henry Grady in his "New
South" speech of 1886. Indeed, its basic civilization waned
slowly and even in the twentieth century there remained vestiges of the Old South.

The part of the Old South that passed away most quickly

after the Civil War was its aristocracy, for it was based largely on slavery and the large plantation. An aristocracy must have not only an economic and governmental base, but like the honor system in colleges, it must have also a tradition, an *esprit de corps*. The Civil War, and perhaps even more the Northern attempt at the reconstruction of the South, destroyed not only the economic sub-structure of the aristocracy, but extinguished the vital spirit, the pride, the confidence, the *elan* of the upper class. One of the tragedies of this dark period in Southern history was that the reconstruction policy of the Northern radicals deprived the Southern people of the leadership of their most experienced and intelligent men at a time when they were the most desperately needed. The "iron-clad oath" and the Fourteenth Amendment, in attempting to punish the Confederate leaders, prevented the natural leaders of the people from participating in the task of restoring order and stability to Southern society. Edgar Gardner Murphy, one of the non-political leaders and reformers of the New South, pointed out in his volume *The Present South* (1903) the folly of the Radical Republicans in excluding from having any part in the reconstruction of their section the class of whites that was most generously disposed toward the freedmen, the men of responsibility in their communities, "the representatives of the aristocracy, the men who were the heirs of the broader and nobler traditions of the South."

Among these representatives of the aristocracy and heirs of the tradition of *noblesse oblige* were Colonel Thomas Dabney, the aristocratic Virginia planter who had settled on the Mississippi plantation Burleigh, and the Creole historian Charles Gayarré. Colonel Dabney was an especially tragic example of the fate that befell many of the aristocracy of the old regime. He was reduced to such poverty that, though seventy years old, he did the family washing. But the individual who pre-eminently illustrated the passing of the old Southern aristocracy, and with it, the waning of the distinctive qualities and attitudes toward life of the Southerners before the war was Charles Gayarré. From the close of the war until his death in 1895, at the age of ninety, he struggled heroically and with great dignity against the poverty and deprivation that were the aftermath of the war. Gayarré is important not simply as an emblem of the Old South culture but because he was highly articulate and discerning; his letters, public lectures, and magazine articles of the post-war period present a critique of the rise of the "New South" and a threnody for the waning of the Old South civilization.

For sixteen years after the war Gayarré was able to continue to live at Roncal, his plantation near New Orleans, and here Grace King visited him when she was a girl fifteen years old. In her *Memories of a Southern Woman of Letters* she has described the utter peace and quiet of the little brown cottage of the Creole historian set in a park of noble trees. When the city girl asked why there were no chickens in the yard, Mrs. Gayarré replied: "The Judge will have no chickens about him, with roosters crowing in the morning to disturb sleep, and hens with their noisy cackling around the house!" Inside the unpretentious cottage were rosewood furniture, French paintings, portraits of his ancestors and one of himself painted when he was a young man in Paris. The face of the portrait, wrote Miss King, "was of great intellectual beauty, with high forehead, clear blue eyes, slightly thinning dark hair, a mouth of slightly ironic lips. It was the portrait of an aristocrat and literaturer."

During the hard times of the post-war readjustment the Judge was forced to sell Roncal and move to an apartment in New Orleans. On January 23, 1867, he wrote to Evert Duyckinck in New York that the South was "getting wild about manufactures," and that his plantation, 84 miles from New Orleans, was on a railroad and had a water power site, and he wished to attract Northern capital and to employ a Yankee to develop it. On August 20 of the same year he wrote to his

New York friend that Yankees had told him that if Roncal, with its six hundred acres, were located in the North it would be worth $500,000, but here, he commented, it was hardly worth a cent. But even before the loss of Roncal in 1881, he burned his accumulation of papers, and one by one sold his artistic treasures and his exquisite French furniture to provide money to sustain life. As late as 1885 he was trying to obtain money by writing to the city editor of the *Picayune* that he would like to "dispose of" a dagger of 1814 that belonged to one of Lafitte's pirates, as well as a manuscript letter of Don Alexandro O'Reilly and one of the noted Spanish governor Bernardo Galvez.

After the Civil War, Gayarré had again attempted to re-enter politics. In 1866 he was a delegate to the Union Democratic Party Convention in Philadelphia. In the following year he became a candidate for the United States Senate but in the balloting in the legislature he was defeated by one vote. During the turbulent Reconstruction period he quietly supported the Democratic ticket, though in his autobiography he said that he had disapproved of some of the candidates and some of the means adopted by his party to win elections. In 1882 he wrote an earnest letter to President Grant urging him to use his influence against the corruption and illegal measures of the carpetbag government in Louisiana, but the passive president replied that reform was up to the state and not to the federal government.

At last, when the Democrats came into power with the election of Cleveland in 1884, he tried to obtain a federal appointment to the naval office of the port of New Orleans. In his quest he wrote to George Bancroft the historian, who had been a Democratic Secretary of the Navy before the war, enlisting his aid. He declared that he had been "a regular Democrat" but that he rested his application on being a Southern man of letters, observing that Northern authors had been recognized and appointed to federal office. But he was unsuccessful, as he had been in an earlier application to President Hayes, and Grace King in her sketch of Gayarré, commented, "And history demands also that the fact be not omitted, that, twice an applicant for an insignificant position, in the gift of the President of the United States by two different Presidents, negroes were preferred to him." To Paul Hamilton Hayne, the South Carolina poet, he explained why he was passed over in federal appointments; "I belong to no ring, to no association of any kind; I am not a professional patriot. I do not steal, drink whiskey, chew tobacco, stuff ballot boxes, nor command the votes of a thousand bog trotters. Better buy a lottery ticket. Washington nowadays could not be elected or appointed, if alive, turnkey to jailbirds."

He met adversity philosophically, saying, "C'est la vie!" On one occasion he declined to give a lecture, explaining that he was too poor to buy suitable clothes to appear on the public platform. He tried to practice law in New Orleans, and between 1873 and 1877 he held the post of reporter of the Supreme Court and published four volumes of the decisions of the Court. He sought to earn money by writing articles for the Northern magazines, but few of his literary productions were accepted. He was able, however, to secure the publication of two novels, neither of which was successful, *Fernando de Lemos* (1872), in which he gave an account of his education at the College of Orleans and *Aubert Dubayet, or the Two Sister Republics* (1882), as well as an earlier comedy, *Doctor Bluff in Russia.*

In 1873 at the request of the editor of the *North American Review*, Gayarré published an article (Vol. 125, Nov.-Dec. pp. 472-98) in which he presented his views of "The Southern Question." The Old South, he said was "a singular compound of aristrocracy and democracy" — slavery produced a democracy of whites; in contrast with society in the North, the white mechanic employed by the planter dined with the master's family, as did the itinerant peddler. No white man was sent to the kitchen to eat with the slaves. At the same time the South had a genuine aristocracy, born with the instinct of command and characterized by self-possession; the North, on the other hand, treated its lower white class as inferiors and its aristocracy, composed of merchants, manufacturers, brokers and bankers, was spurious. The ideal blend in the Old South of aristocracy and white democracy, he observed, had passed away, and the North and the West had succeeded in reducing Southern society to their own level.

But blood will tell, he maintained; the Caucasian race was destined gradually to conquer the globe. He was one of the early exponents in the South of social Darwinism, to whose theory of evolution he referred in his article as maintaining the doctrine of the survival of the fittest. The two races, Negro and Caucasian, he asserted, were as different as day and night and could never fuse into a natural and harmonious whole. He pointed out that the races were every day drawing apart, save in the Catholic church. The Negroes were separating into segregated churches; the old kindly feeling of the whites toward the Negro of slavery days was vanishing; black nurses no longer were allowed to kiss and spank white children as they had done in the old regime; Negro servants refused to sleep in the houses of their employers as in former days. His remedies for the evils of Reconstruction were simple; home rule for the Southern states, white supremacy, strict segregation of the races, and removal of the Negro question from national politics. At the same time he advocated that educational opportunities be given to the Negro equal to those enjoyed by the whites. "Today," he concluded somberly, "the South is desperately poor but also it has been sick so long that it is impossible to entertain any hope for a prompt convalescence."

Especially revealing of the mood of Gayarré and of the upper class of the deep South was the conversation that he had with Edward King in this year. The Creole historian was so despondent that he told the Northern journalist that "among his immense acquaintance in Louisiana he did not know a single person who would not leave the state if means were at hand." Gayarré portrayed his native state as beset by manifold evils — many "lovely plantations" were abandoned because their owners could not pay taxes on them; taxes, indeed, were so enormous that business as well as farming was depressed; Southern ladies who were wealthy before the war were now "washing" for their daily bread; the state was ruled by an ignorant and corrupt legislature; in one single legislature, he declared, there were fifty-five members who could not read and write. Twelve years later the situation of the white people of the state, he thought, had not greatly improved; he wrote then to Bancroft that the people of Louisiana were so disgusted with the frauds practiced at the ballot box and the corruption of the government that in the last general election only a third of the registered voters had gone to the polls. In New Orleans there was a stagnation of business; the merchants and businessmen were doing only 50 per cent as much business as during the previous year. Only the eating houses, drinking shops, and "certain nameless establishments" were prospering.

In 1885 when Gayarré was eighty years old, he appeared once more in print as a defender of the South. George Washington Cable, the New Orleans novelist, had published in January 1885 in the *Century Magazine* an article entitled "The Freedmen's Case in Equity" that aroused much resentment in the South. In this article the New Orleans romancer had taken the Southern people to task for their unjust treatment of the Negro. He had advocated that the Negroes should be granted political equality and that they should not be segregated in schools, concerts, theatres, trains, or waiting rooms. The weakness of Cable's article was its vagueness in defining the distinction between civil equality, which he demanded for the Negro, and social equality which he did not propose.

Up to this point, Gayarré and Cable seemed to have enjoyed good relations, indicated by letters preserved in Tulane University Library. Gayarré had, in a letter of October 27, 1880, consulted Cable on the ways to secure a publisher in New York for a work entitled "The Blacks of Louisiana," part of which he had published in the New Orleans *Times-Democrat*. He now proposed to write the history of the black race in Louisiana down to the contemporary period. He thought that such a work would appeal to the Northern white people as well as to the Negroes and might be used as a text book in the Negro schools, "and why not," he asked, "since it is our constitutional duty and our intention to educate them."

Now, five years later, he was moved to reply to Cable's indictment of the South in the New Orleans *Times-Democrat* on January 8 and 11, 1885. He remarked that, though he had read the article three times, with extreme fatigue, he still was uncertain as to what it meant. "Mr. Cable seems to wish," Gayarré wrote, "to bring together, by every possible means, the blacks and whites in the most familiar and closest friction everywhere, in every imaginable place of resort, save the private parlor and the private bed chamber, into which, for the present, a disagreeable intrusion may not be permitted." With incisive irony Gayarré attacked Cable for his lofty assumption of moral superiority over his fellow citizens and his libels of the Southern people. In his autobiography, Gayarré states that his demolition of Cable's article had won for him the appellation of "Champion of the South" from several Southern periodicals.

In the same year that Gayarré won the sobriquet of "Champion of the South," he also became the defender of the historic reputation of the Louisiana Creoles. The Creoles had greatly resented Cable's portrayal of them in his short stories *Old Creole Days* (1879) and his two novels *The Grandissimes* (1880) and *Dr. Sevier* (1884). Gayarré, at first, refrained from any public criticism of Cable's fiction. When the New

Orleans *Times-Democrat* asked him to review *The Grandissimes* he refused, and when Cable asked him to reconsider
his decision he replied that he would do so if the novelist
could name two Creole families with whom he was intimately
acquainted. The novelist could not do so. Cable, instead of
Gayarré, was asked to write the article on the Creoles for the
ninth edition of the *Encyclopaedia Britannica* (1884), and also
in the same year the novelist published some articles in the
Century about Creole history as well as a popular historical
work entitled *The Creoles of Louisiana*. In this book Cable
referred to the treachery of General James Wilkinson with the
Spanish authorities, which caused his grandson, also named
James Wilkinson, to accuse Cable of slander. In defending
himself Cable declared that he had derived his information
from Gayarré's history of Louisiana. Thus Gayarré was drawn
into a controversy both with the grandson of Wilkinson and
with Cable; he declared in the *Times-Democrat* of May 20,
1885, "Cable copied my statements and published them as
his own." In addition to his resentment over plagiarism,
Gayarré felt that Cable's *The Creoles of Louisiana,* as well as
his colorful fiction, misrepresented the historical Creoles.

Accordingly, the indignant Creole historian delivered a lec-
ture in French in New Orleans, entitled "La Race Latine en
Louisiane" and later one in English entitled "The Creoles of
History and the Creoles of Romance." Admitting that of
Cable's novels, he had read only *The Grandissimes,* he proceeded to show that the author was guilty of four major mis-
representations of the Creoles; (1) the true Creoles spoke
French, but the novelist had portrayed them as speaking a
jargon of pigeon French; (2) Cable had insinuated that the
Creoles had Negro blood in their veins; (3) he implied also
that many of them were descended from French prostitutes;
and (4) he portrayed the Creoles as stupid, effete, and base
in character. In these eloquent lectures Gayarré contributed
to the creation of a glamorous legend of the Creoles very much

as Thomas Nelson Page in his novels and short stories created
a romantic stereotype of plantation life in Virginia before
the war.

The passing of the years did not lift the gloom from
Gayarré's spirit. His strong condemnation of the treatment of
the South by the Reconstruction measures was reflected in the
letters that he wrote to Paul Hamilton Hayne. These letters
are preserved in Duke University Library. In 1885 a remarkable friendship developed between the two men; Gayarré was
eighty years old and Hayne, then living in extreme poverty
in a cabin near Augusta, Georgia, was young enough to be
Gayarré's son. The incident that brought about this beautiful
friendship was Gayarré's public condemnation of George
Washington Cable's article in the *Century Magazine,* "The
Freedmen's Case in Equity." The South Carolina poet praised
Gayarré profusely for his defense of the South. On the other
hand, he was dissatisfied with Henry W. Grady's reply to the
Cable indictment, entitled "In Plain Black and White," published in the *Century Magazine* in the same year. Hayne considered it to be too moderate in tone. Though Hayne and
Gayarré never saw each other, they developed what the octo-
genarian man of letters described as "an intuitive congenial-
ity." Hayne sent to his new-found friend volumes of his poetry,
and the latter responded by sending his history of Louisiana;
they praised each others works and exchanged photographs.

Hayne sought to advance the appreciation of Gayarré in
the South by publishing two articles in *The Southern Bivouac*
of Louisville, Kentucky, "Charles Gayarré, the Statesman"
(June 1886), and "Charles Gayarré, the Author" (July
1886). In the first of these, he pictured the Creole historian
as the exemplar of "a lineage stainless and well nigh princely,"
and wrote that his motto had ever been *noblesse oblige.* He
severely rebuked the people of Louisiana for the callous neglect
of their most eminent citizen; they had failed to reward him
with a political office that would enable him to keep the wolf

from his doorway, although the Democratic party of the state was beholden to him for incalculable services, and he was still physically and mentally vigorous. While he was composing this article Hayne wrote to Gayarré, "I am going to give your Louisianians 'particular hell' because of their conduct toward you." In the second article, which he wrote in his last days while he was struggling with the fatal disease of tuberculosis, he praised his friend's literary works, especially his history of Louisiana, which he observed "combined exhaustive research, logical arrangement and a graphic, picturesque, scholarly style." Gayarré, in turn, after the death of Hayne, wrote an appreciation of the Carolina poet, entitled "Paul Hayne, Painted by Himself," but he could not find a publisher for it.

But Gayarré and Hayne represented only one aspect of the waning of the Old South culture, namely, the passing of the older Southern aristocracy — they were indeed the last roses of summer. Charles R. Anderson in his article about their literary friendship and correspondence has aptly called them the "Last Literary Cavaliers" of the South. The historian, Charles Colcock Jones, Jr., of Georgia, and William Hand Browne, editor of the *Southern Magazine* at Baltimore, were also especially vocal in urging Southerners to hold fast to the old traditions. Browne wrote to Gayarré on August 8, 1872 (MS in Louisiana State University Department of Archives and Manuscripts), seeking to enlist his aid in forming a "Southern Literary Guild," for the promotion of literature in the South and for "the preservation of what is good and noble of our old Southern customs and ways; and the resistance of all pernicious innovations."

There was, however, a younger and more effective generation of supporters of "the Lost Cause" who adapted themselves to the changed times after the war and were able to make satisfactory careers for themselves. The late Professor William B. Hesseltine made a study of the careers of 585 civil and military leaders of the Confederacy who were able to reestab-

lish themselves after the debacle. These "leaders" were mostly
between thirty and fifty years of age when the war ended, and
in 1890, 50 per cent of them were alive. He concluded that
"of 656 prominent Confederates who lived long enough to
make postwar readjustments, only 71 failed to recover a sub-
stantial portion of the position and prestige they had enjoyed
at the Confederacy's peak." Especially interesting were the
post-war political careers of the former Confederate military
leaders. The federal Amnesty Act of 1872 pardoned all but
about five hundred of the high Confederate civil officers and
permitted them to be elected to office. There were 73 leaders
of the former Confederacy, the so-called "rebel brigadiers,"
who sat in Congress after the war, whose careers were distinguished by their conservative votes and their "quietness,"
or lack of sectional defiance. Of the 585 former Confederate
leaders, 418 after the war held elective or appointive office
in the state, local, or federal governments. The elite group
of the defeated Confederacy — the men of brains, ambition,
and energy — could not be repressed for long. In addition to
the group of politicians, the 585 "leaders," according to Professor Hesseltine's count, furnished to the New South 292
lawyers, 193 planters or farmers, 73 railroad officials, 39 merchants, 34 industrialists, 25 insurance men, and 23 bankers.
Among the prominent Confederate leaders who prospered,
after a period of readjustment, were General Pierre Beauregard, who had left the Confederate Army with only $1.15 in
cash, and General Jubal Early, who had fled to Mexico but returned to a law practice in Lynchburg, Virginia, and eventually joined Beauregard in a lucrative connection with the
notorious Louisiana Lottery.

Perhaps the most admirable of the former Confederate
leaders who made new careers for themselves were those military officers who became professors, presidents of colleges, and
founders of academies. Heading this list was Robert E. Lee,
who served as president of Washington College (the name

was changed after his death to Washington and Lee), who was succeeded as president by his ineffective son, Major General George Washington Custis Lee. Other prominent ex-Confederate military officers who served as presidents of Southern colleges or universities were Colonel William Preston Johnston, president of Louisiana State University and Tulane University, General D. H. Hill, president of Arkansas Industrial University and later of Middle Georgia Military and Agricultural College, General Josiah Gorgas, president of the University of Alabama, Confederate congressman and Colonel Jabez L. M. Curry, president of Richmond College, Lieutenant General A. P. Stewart, called "Old Straight" by the soldiers, chancellor of the University of Mississippi, and Admiral Franklin Buchanan, president of Maryland Agricultural College. Confederate officers who served as professors in Southern colleges included Lieutenant General Kirby Smith and Brigadier General Francis Asbury Shoup at the University of the South Sewanee, Tennessee, Robert Lewis Dabney at Hampden-Sydney, Raphael Semmes, briefly at Louisiana State University, Brigadier General George Washington Rains at the University of Georgia, and Brigadier General E. P. Alexander at the University of South Carolina.

The political activities of this generation of ex-Confederates who "redeemed" the South from the rule of the carpetbaggers, scalawags, and their Negro supporters lie beyond the limits of this study. It is a story that has been told and retold, usually with partisan bias, most recently by the revisionist school of historians. Indeed, the controversial nature of its study has been appropriately called "the dark and bloody ground of Reconstruction historiography." This account of the social and cultural life of the South during the twenty years from 1860 to 1880 is concerned, rather, with the slow and gradual change of attitudes and customs of the Southern people. The emphasis is not on the forces that were creating a new structure of society but on the tenacity of the old forces and ideas rooted in the soil of the ante-bellum South. A later volume is planned to deal with the progressive forces, with the rise of the "New South" between 1880 and 1900. Even the "New South," which Henry W. Grady, Bishop Atticus G. Haygood, and the new breed of Southern industrialists hailed, retained more of the Old South than it created. The Old South, indeed, waned slowly and with a decidedly uneven time lag in different areas of the South. The "New South" was primarily a product of the few cities and large towns — notably Atlanta, Birmingham, Chattanooga — while in the country and small villages, where the vast majority of the people lived, much of the spirit of the Old South persisted for a long time.

Most of the cities repaired the war damage rapidly and developed the spirit of enterprise, an eagerness to attract Northern capital, and a desire to create a "New South" on the basis of industrialism. Atlanta, where Henry Grady's paper, the *Constitution,* was preaching the gospel of forgetting the Confederate past, reconciling the South to the Northern conquerors, and adopting the Yankee principles of hustle, shrift, and the unrelenting pursuit of money, was an outstanding example of change. It was becoming a city of self-made men, of millionaires — an ugly, utilitarian town, Sir George Campbell found it to be in 1878 — "a new brick-built town, with no trees in the streets, but abundant mud." The symbols of its departure from Old South traditions were its principal hotel, the Kimball House, and a vulgar Opera House built by a Northern opportunist and corruptionist, who sold the latter to the state as a Capitol Building after the seat of government was removed to Atlanta.

In the changing conditions of the so-called "New South" the distinctive qualities of the old plantation aristocracy began to wane with the gradual disappearance of the plantation as a dominant feature of the South's economy. But it is a mistake to assume that the Civil War resulted in the quick passing of the large plantation. It is true that many of the original owners lost their lands because of crushing debts, inability to hire labor, the lack of money to pay taxes, especially the unjust federal tax on cotton, and the foreclosure of mortgages. Also, some of the old and discouraged planters sold their lands to Northern men who anticipated golden profits from buying up or leasing Southern plantations cheaply. John Hay, Lincoln's secretary, for instance, bought an orange plantation in Florida, but it proved an unprofitable investment; Whitelaw Reid in 1865 invested his money in three plantations in Concordia Parish, Louisiana, opposite Natchez, but he too lost his investment. Thereafter he changed his radical views concerning the Negro. One of the most interesting of these Northern men who moved into the South to make profits from farming or business was Albion W. Tougee, a former officer in an Ohio regiment, who established a nursery and small plantation near Greensboro, North Carolina. His business venture, however, declined rapidly when he became a carpetbagger in politics, and he was forced to sell at a great loss. Indeed, after he was elected by the Republicans to the office of a Superior Court Judge and vigorously prosecuted the Ku Klux Klan, he was ostracized by his community and departed for the West, describing his unhappy experiences in North Carolina in a book that he published in 1879 as *A Fool's Errand.*

The statistics published by the Census Bureau in 1880 obscured the fact that the plantations survived in considerable numbers in many parts of the South. According to its reports, between 1860 and 1880 the number of small farms increased tremendously and the average landholding was reduced from 365 acres to 157 acres, but the census takers in counting the number of agricultural units made no distinction between owners of farms or plantations and tenants. Actually, a large number of the individual farms they included belonged to plantation owners who operated their extensive tracts of land by using tenants. Roger W. Shugg in an article in the *Journal of Southern History* (August, 1937) entitled "Survival of the

Plantation System in Louisiana," maintained that in Louisiana the plantation system not only survived after the war but actually expanded. In the two decades from 1860 to 1880 he noted "the number of landholdings multiplied 89 per cent, and of plantations, 287 per cent, while the number of farms actually decreased 14 per cent. Until 1880, in short, the larger properties encroached upon the smaller, but after that date farming developed faster than planting. Yet the increase of great estates throughout the country had such a cumulative effect that although Louisiana had contained more farms than plantations in 1860, it was dominated by agrarian monopoly in 1900 when its proportion of absentee ownership and overseer management was the largest in the South, and highest in the entire United States except for Wyoming." There were special reasons why the large plantation continued to exist in Louisiana; it was a sugar producing state, and the culture of sugar cane required unusually large amounts of capital to keep the dykes and draining ditches in proper condition and to maintain the equipment for turning cane juice into sugar. There continued, moreover, after the war a feeling that to own a plantation was a matter of prestige and the planters held on tenaciously to the land partly for this reason.

Nevertheless, though the plantation system survived in Louisiana, it was able to do so only because planters could borrow money on the basis of crop liens from New Orleans bankers and commission houses. Many of the old owners, however, did not retain their properties; their plantations were acquired by corporations or by shrewd furnishing merchants or enterprising men of humble birth. Such a man was Leon Godchaux, a French immigrant who had begun his career as a peddler among the plantations, then became a merchant in New Orleans, and in 1862 bought his first sugar plantation; thereafter, he continued to add to his holdings so that at his death in 1896 he owned twelve plantations and had laid the foundations of the Godchaux sugar empire. Some of the large ante-bellum sugar plantation owners such as Duncan Kenner, the Minors, John Burnside, and Andrew McCollam survived the war as prosperous planters, but Shugg has observed "Almost half the sugar planters in 1869 bore names that slaveholding families would not have recognized."

Among these later planters was Henry Clay Warmoth, a carpetbagger who served as the Republican governor of the state from 1868 to 1872. In the following year Warmoth entered the ranks of the sugar planters by acquiring part ownership of the great Magnolia plantation from its ante-bellum owner, Effingham Lawrence, who was so harassed by debts that he took this Northern adventurer into partnership to save the plantation.

Outside the sugar producing region a considerable number of large plantations in fertile soil districts also survived. One of these was Ventosa, a 5,000 acre cotton and corn plantation in the Roanoke River valley of eastern North Carolina, owned by the Clark family of Highland Scotch origin. Before the war it had been cultivated by 200 slaves, and a visitor saw on one day seventy slaves ploughing its fields. After the war the young heir, Walter Clark, returned from the Confederate Army to find the beautiful mansion burned to the ground, the slaves and stock gone, and the fields covered with weeds and briars. Possessing great energy and intelligence, he set about to restore the plantation, borrowed money from commission houses in Norfolk and Baltimore, recruited labor from many of the former slaves of the plantation, and continued to operate the plantation with tenants from his near-by law office in Halifax and later from Raleigh until his death in 1924. The Barrow plantation in Georgia was another example of the survival of the plantation. Although the Census Bureau counted it as 24 farms because it was operated by 24 tenants, most of whom were former slaves who had stayed on the land, it was owned by the old master and really was a large decentralized plantation.

The author described in a journal, kept during a research trip into the deep South in the summer of 1935, a large plantation near the village of Lowndesboro, Alabama, on which vestiges of the Old South remained. He visited the Dixon home — an imposing classical building on the outside but very disappointing within. The master was a hale, weather-beaten man, bald-headed, and very jovial. He boasted of his forty fox hounds of the Walker breed, and he blew his horn, made from an antler, which set his dogs to baying and yelping. He said that he owned 6,000 acres of land. He was proud of his small son, seven or eight years old, a sun-tanned little fellow, who had just killed his first bird in flight. He also had a daughter, who was entering Goucher College in the fall. Yet there was an unpleasant side to "Bob" Dixon — he had killed, the author was told, several Negroes, and he acted as though slavery had never been abolished.

Although many plantations remained after the war, the spirit, discipline, and efficiency of the ante-bellum plantation was gone because of the abolition of slavery and the rise of the tenant system. This system marked an improvement over slavery for the Negro, but it gradually encompassed thousands of white yeomen who had owned their farms before the war and it impaired their sense of independence and manly spirit. Moreover, the turmoil and violence of Southern society following the surrender at Appomattox seriously injured the integrity of character and the moral tone of the post-war generation. The political corruption of the period has been thoroughly described by the various historians of the Reconstruction period, often in the darkest colors, particularly by Claude Bowers in *The Tragic Era,* but the revisionists have shown that political corruption in the South during Reconstruction has been greatly exaggerated and that Southern politicians as well as the carpet-baggers participated in it.

A subject that has not been investigated so thoroughly was the growth of private and commercial dishonesty in the period.

In Mississippi Trowbridge was told in 1865 by the assistant commissioner of the Freedmen's Bureau that two-thirds of the Negroes were cheated out of their wages by white employers and that some Southerners operated on the basis that honesty was an obligation to be exercised only toward white people. Not only native Southerners, but Northern speculators, corrupt Freedmen's Bureau agents, and small Jewish merchants who flocked into the South, preyed upon the naive Negroes. Sidney Andrews reported that "the Rebellion has sapped commercial honor and integrity" in the South. Laura Comer, the Northern-born wife of a planter who owned plantations in Georgia and Alabama, wrote in her diary (manuscript in the Southern Collection, University of North Carolina) on November 16, 1867, that she had been afraid since the war to trust anyone; "all nice sense of honor," she observed, "seems to have been swept away by the war."

The stresses of a long war and the disorganization of society that followed greatly impaired the outstanding virtues of the society of the Old South, the hospitality of the people, their high sense of honor, their chivalry, and their elegant courtesy. In Louisiana Gayarré lamented that the planters had become so poor that they were no longer able, and had even lost the spirit, to maintain "the grand, unbounded hospitality once so characteristic of the South." Dennett, travelling on horseback, was frequently refused a night's lodging and food, because the people themselves had so little to eat and were ashamed for a stranger to witness their deprivation. As Edward King was gathering material in 1873 for his book *The Great South,* he met in Vicksburg a Mississippi planter who seemed to him the *beau ideal* of the Southern gentlemen. "Colonel Vick, the present representative of the family [that founded Vicksburg]," he wrote, "is a specimen of the true, noble-looking men grown in the Mississippi Valley, — six feet in stature, erect and stately, witty, with the charming courtesy of the old school." He met also some old Negroes who had caught an air of dignity and courtesy from their masters and displayed the beautiful manners which became a lost art to the succeeding generations of Negroes.

As Gayarré lived on into the era of the New South he observed the gradual disappearance of those qualities that had distinguished the Old South. Moreover, he was saddened to see the plague of ugliness, the complete disregard for beauty that the commercial spirit of the new age was exhibiting. It had brought to the fair land of Louisiana, to the delightful, unique city of New Orleans, a mania for removing old landmarks, for tearing down attractive old homes to make way for so-called "progress," to erect on their ruins ugly, utilitarian buildings. Nevertheless, the Creole aristocrat had shown in his historical works that he believed in true progress. He recognized also that some of what he called the old "castellated" notions of the South must pass away, for they were not suited to a new age in which Southerners were seeking to restore prosperity to their section by the introduction of industrialism.

The "Chivalrous Southrons" that De Forest observed in South Carolina after the war were a fast vanishing breed. They were a peculiar product of the Old South, the "high-toned gentlemen," who prided themselves on their sense of honor and who were quick to resent insults. Walter Hines Page noted a shining example of the Old South sense of honor in the Bingham School at Mebane, North Carolina, which he attended when he was twelve years old. Colonel Robert Bingham, the headmaster, replied to the plea of a parent whose son had been dismissed for cheating: "I could not keep the honour of the school — I could not even keep the boys if he were to return. They would appeal to their parents and most of them would be called home. They are the flower of the South, Sir." The students themselves gave a social rank to the members of the school, according the highest rank to the son of a general or a high officer of the Confederacy, then to the son of a governor or judge, next to the son of an Episcopalian clergyman, followed in rank by the son of a Presbyterian preacher. Page, whose father was a Methodist and a Unionist and had no military title, had to win his way by the merits of his personality alone. Also Colonel Richard Malcolm Johnston in his Pen Lucy School at Baltimore and Robert E. Lee, as president of Washington College, based discipline on the appeal to the sense of honor of the students and treated them as gentlemen.

Many of the younger ex-Confederates, who adapted themselves to the changed conditions of the post-war South preserved, nevertheless, some of the distinctive elements of the Old South culture. One of these was Walter Clark, who in his later career was prominent in North Carolina as a progressive leader and Chief Justice of the state supreme court. Born on the great plantation of Ventosa on the Roanoke River, with its 5,000 acres and 200 slaves, Clark was the heir to an aristocratic tradition. The Old South aristocrats had valued a military education, and young Walter was sent to Tew's Military Academy at Hillsboro, North Carolina, whose principal, a West Point graduate, modeled it after West Point. In 1861 when North Carolina mobilized its citizen soldiers, Clark, though only fourteen years old, served as drillmaster at Raleigh and when he ended his military career shortly after fighting in the battle of Bentonville in March 1865 he held the rank of lieutenant colonel. All through the war he was attended, as were many of the young aristocratic soldiers, by a faithful body-servant, "Neverson."

After the war he demonstrated on two occasions particularly the continuing influence of Old South traditions upon him. In 1871 he challenged to a duel the writer of a communication in a Norfolk, Virginia, newspaper whom he thought had reflected upon his honor as a gentleman. During the following year he attended at Burlington, North Carolina, a romantic tournament of knights and their fair ladies, such as were held before the war, and here he met "Miss Sudie Graham," the daughter of a prominent Whig politician before the war, whom he courted and married. Also, throughout his life he held fast to the orthodox religion that was the faith of the generation of Southerners that fought in the Confederate Army. His family were devout Methodists who had employed a young minister to preach to their slaves, and young Walter, while off at school, wrote to his mother: "I read three chapters of my Bible regularly every day and five or ten every Sunday, like you requested me to do. I go to Sunday School and church and also clean my teeth every morning, and everything else you requested me to do. I have most finished Caesar." As to the ritualistic reading of the Bible by Southerners, Colonel Richard Malcolm Johnston observed in his autobiography that many of the rural Georgians of his youth had read the Bible through, over and over again, and could freely quote passages from it.

The continuity of life in the Southern villages and rural districts after the war was striking. In 1879 Walter Hines Page, one of the young harbingers of the "New South," published an article in the *Atlantic Monthly* entitled "An Old Southern Borough," which described the unbroken tenor of life in the Piedmont village of Hillsboro, North Carolina. Here in this old town, once the colonial capital of North Carolina, there was remarkably little change from the time before the Civil War. Page portrayed the ruling class of old-fashioned Southern gentlemen, quoting Horace and Virgil, reading old-fashioned English authors and the novels of Scott, maintaining the legal correctness of secession, and boasting of the achievements of the South during the Civil War. Twenty years after the South seceded from the Union there remained in Hillsboro the same atmosphere of indolence, the same concern with gossip — the marriages, the fights, and the deaths of the villagers — and the same lack of interest or knowledge of the outside world as had existed before the Civil War. The villagers continued to rely on the Negroes, or "the darkeys," as they called them, to do menial and manual labor as they had before emancipation, nor had they changed the stereotypes that they held before the war concerning the inherent inferiority of the Negro; they practiced a mild paternalism toward the lowly race, but took a keen relish in the idiosyncrasies and humor of the Negroes. They preserved intact the old South's religious faith, its loyalty to family and kin, its romantic etiquette toward women, its hatred of the Yankee, its strong conservative spirit, and its belief in the superiority of the Southern people and their way of life to that of the other residents in the United States, and in fact, in the world. When Page toured the South two years later as a newspaper correspondent, he noted the unprogressive nature of Southern society, the general shiftlessness of the people, the tobacco chewing, stick-whittling loafers at the village stores and railroad stations, the unpainted, dilapidated houses, the old-fashioned methods of agriculture, and the lack of fresh ideas or of an enterprising spirit. Even the Southern dogs, he commented, looked old-fashioned.

Ten years after Page described the somnolent Old-South atmosphere of Hillsboro, Edwin A. Alderman together with Charles D. McIver of North Carolina traveled through the state on a speaking tour to arouse the people to support public education. Alderman was a graduate of the University of North Carolina, a handsome, eloquent man, and a true crusader for stirring the people from their lethargy to establish a good public school system. From July 1 to approximately the middle of December 1889, he kept two manuscript notebooks (now deposited in the Alderman Library of the University of Virginia) in which he made comments not only on the school situation in the various counties that he visited but on public opinion, politics, the Negro, crime, and social and economic conditions.

Alderman's observations of conditions in some of the western counties reveal dark shadows of provincialism and backwardness. In Orange County where the University and the famous Bingham prep school were located, he found "the direst ignorance among the masses." Of Polk County, he wrote: "People are inert and work very little. Shoot squirrels and eat fruit and work about one-third of their time." He described Wilkes County as "a very ignorant county—largely Republican, 600 majority. No negro school teachers—white men teach negro schools. More bastardy in this county between white folks than I ever heard of, common as stealing in the East." He was amused by Davidson County: "Davidson is a queer county. It was stated to me by responsible parties that there were 500 purchasable votes in the county ranging in price from 50¢ to $20.00." (Such low political morality was perhaps an aftermath of the Reconstruction period and the struggle of Southern whites to eliminate the Negro vote.) In Alleghany County, he observed, "the mass of the whites are poor and ignorant. They do not need to work very hard in order to live. Bastardy and murder common in this county. 42 homicides since '65 and not a single Execution." Hendersonville was described as "a South Carolina town" — the people traded with the latter state and read its newspapers. In politics, it had a Republican majority, and during the Civil War it had sent two companies of soldiers to the Federal army.

As the young crusader traveled through these rural communities, he noted the social conditions that retarded the development of free public schools. He was enough of a realist to see how influential were the leading men in each community, the men of wealth and property, in deciding the question of voting taxes for schools. He wrote in his notes on Henderson County, for example: "If M. E. Toms, Dr. C. Few, & W. A. Smith could be reached they could change the aspects of affairs in Henderson County" by securing a favorable vote for raising taxes for schools. Some of the most enlightened of these key men, such as the great industrialist Julian Carr in Durham, gave him their cordial support but others were hostile to increased taxation for school purposes. To the selfishness of wealthy taxpayers he ascribed the decline of public schools in Lenoir County: "The town [of Kinston] once had a good graded school but let it die — now the negros own the former graded school building and the whites use a hut. In 1883, 500 white children attended school — now in 1890 about 150, — considerable opposition to schools. The Property men as usual run things and kill off all school aspirations." Alderman also recognized that the development of industries and the opening up of isolated communities by railroads furnished wealth and ultimately stimulus to the establishment of an adequate school system. Yet he observed sadly the cultural lag between the rise of manufactures and the improvement of mental and spiritual conditions. Concerning the town of Concord, he commented, "Concord has the largest factory in the state, street cars, electric lights, & water works. Improvement in schools generally comes last." He jotted down also the notation that Alamance County had fifteen cotton mills, thirteen of which were owned by the Holts, yet that the county had deteriorated educationally in the last two years.

Another weighty factor which interfered with the progress of the public school movement was the existence of numerous factional quarrels and religious dissensions in the little villages. He cited the case of Brevard in Transylvania County, a county where there was no school lasting more than four months in the year. The school of Brevard was conducted in a building used by the Baptist Church and the Masonic lodge. The town was torn by intense religious differences, "all that brood of troubles that beset small localities. Baptists predominate, the people lazy — poorly governed. Railroads and schools would change the state of affairs." The town of Jefferson had a good schoolhouse but no teacher "owing to local friction and inability to agree. This folly kills the intellectual life of many children." He found that in Cabarrus County "church differences as usual have fought against the welfare of the children." The hard shell Baptists, he declared, were opposed to all education. In Montgomery County the teacher training institute was injured by a large "Revival" distracting the people. He commented caustically on another occasion: "Politics and religion never fail to *draw*."

Often Alderman spoke before apathetic audiences under conditions that were extremely depressing to the young orator. At Jefferson in Ashe County where there had been no school for six years, he wrote: "I did my best but couldn't stir things much. What between crying babies, squealing pigs, badly behaved children, Sam, the village idiot, and an ill-conditioned superintendent (a large, red-faced whisky-drinker) my oratorical task was heavy." The gloom of his notes are occasionally relieved by such bits of humor as above and by his statement about Washington in the eastern part of the state, as "a pleasant little town full of pretty women. All the women along these rivers are inclined to Embonpoint. Why is this?" Forest City in Rutherford County he described as "a queer little place two miles long and ten feet wide," inhabited by four hundred people. Of one North Carolina teacher he met, he commented, "He could easily walk boldly into a comic novel."

But pathos rather than amusement dominated his feelings as he observed quaint and backward conditions in isolated communities. Concerning the unfitness of the teachers, chiefly ungainly country lads who taught school for three months a year and farmed for nine months, he wrote: "What encouragement have they either in salary or influence. Neither have they, as a rule, had any showing in life. I have them to write for me, as an exercise, a brief autobiographical sketch, and I am touched to the heart by the monotonous, sickening story of lack of opportunity for mental development."

Furthermore, the schoolhouses were frequently miserable structures — log cabins, or dilapidated frame houses with the window panes out of them and with no desks. The parents often took little interest in the improvement of the schools or in sending their children regularly to such schools as were available. Alderman describes the situation in Pamlico County, an isolated county in the east, which had no courthouse and a poverty-stricken people. The institute was held in "a typical, rickety, cheerless public school house." He counted thirteen panes of glass out of the windows. As he observed the children, he reflected: "The solemn-faced little children of this county haven't much showing in life. A mortal lethargy seems settled over all, what changes a *good* school in every district would bring, Blair's bill would give it. These people know the public schools only to sneer at them so far as I can see and this is not to be marvelled at if a tree shall be judged by its fruits."

In such social atmosphere as described by Alderman, which was not confined to North Carolina but was widespread throughout the rural South, the religion, the social customs and mores, and even some of the political ideas of the Old South lingered. One of the heritages from the society of the Old South was a staunch devotion to states' rights, based partly on state pride. When the Northern journalist John T. Trowbridge journeyed through the South in 1865, he was amazed at the strength of state pride displayed by the inhabitants. Riding in a stagecoach in eastern Virginia, he talked to an expressman, a former soldier in the Confederate army, who told him: "I am a son of Virginia! I was opposed to secession at first, but afterwards I went into it with my whole heart and soul. Do you know what carried me in? State pride, sir! Nothing else in the world. I'd give more for Virginia than for all the rest of the Union put together; and I was bound to go with my state." Trowbridge found that state pride flourished far more strongly in the South than in the North or West. Edward King, who traveled in the South in 1873-74, found that an "overweening pride in the State" continued to exist in the region below the Potomac. "As a rule," he wrote in his travel volume, *The Great South,* "two Southerners traveling in a State remote from that in which they are born find an instant bond of communion in the fact that they are from the same commonwealth." But he accurately predicted that the progressive introduction of railroads would greatly dilute the Southerner's pride in his region, and render him more and more like his bustling fellow-citizen in the North and the West. Even more effective in making the South more like the rest of the country was the great educational awakening that took place after 1900.

Another instance of the survival of pre-Civil War attitudes, as late as the 1880's, was what Thomas B. Alexander has called "persistent Whiggery." Charles Nordhoff, correspondent of the *New York Herald* traveling in the South in 1875, observed "tradition lives longer among the Southern whites than with us," and he cited as evidence the strong feelings of hostility from the past that existed between the revived Whigs and the Democrats. So strong was the inherited distrust and dislike of the old-line Whigs toward the Democrats that in order to secure the cooperation of native white Southerners against the carpetbagger governments it was necessary in some states, notably Louisiana and Virginia, to drop the name "Democratic" and substitute the term "Conservative." Nordhoff noted that the old Southern Whig was a conservative, who was suppressed during the war but came forward after Appomattox to take the lead of the Southern whites.

The survival of the Old South into the twentieth century was sustained by the rise of the cult of "the Lost Cause." This is a story of great social significance that awaits the study of a competent historian, but it cannot be told here. The cult was one of the three "ghosts" that Walter Hines Page said haunted the Southern mind; the others were the ghost of religious orthodoxy and the fear that underlay the dogma of white supremacy. The loyalty of Southerners to the Confederate leaders and heroes continued to be a powerful force in Southern politics until the twentieth century. Sir George Campbell noted in 1878 that Southerners voted for one-armed and one-legged Confederate veterans for office as a means of providing them with some sort of pension. In the Virginia Conservative Convention of 1877, John S. Wise, the son of ex-Governor Henry A. Wise, appealed to Confederate loyalists while withdrawing the name of General William Mahone as a candidate for governor, by declaring: "I am commissioned by the hero of the Crater to appeal to every friend of his in these convention walls to remember his watchword 'Follow Accomac,' and cast his vote for the one-armed hero of the Shenandoah Valley, Colonel F. W. M. Holliday." Southerners developed such an unwavering attitude of voting for Confederate officers and heroes for public office that the candidate without a military record, though of vastly superior ability, had virtually no chance of election against the Confederate brigadier with his venerable white locks and beard, his florid oratory, and his sentimental appeal to Confederate memories. Professor Paul Buck in his *The Road to Reunion* has noted that in 1878 the eight Congressional seats of Alabama were held by eight Confederate veterans; Confederate veterans filled all but one of Georgia's seats in Congress; and in 1883 all five of the Congressmen from Arkansas had fought for "the Lost Cause." Loyalty to "the Lost Cause" was perpetuated especially by the United Daughters of the Confederacy, but it was a sentiment that fitted the romanticism of the region. To some degree the cult arose as a compensation for the bleak years that had followed defeat and for the inferiority complex that the Southern people developed.

The course of the Romantic Movement, which had partly shaped the Old South civilization, flowed unchecked by the Civil War through the remaining years of the nineteenth century. Tennyson was the favorite poet of the post-war generation, and Sir Walter Scott's novels continued to be read. William Alexander Percy in his delightful recollections of his childhood in Mississippi, *Lanterns on the Levee,* records that his aristocratic father, Governor LeRoy Percy, "read *Ivanhoe* once a year all his life long and *The Talisman* almost as frequently."

One of the greatest manifestations of this Old South heritage of romanticism was the cult of Southern Womanhood. In his *Mind of the South* Wilbur J. Cash explained the cult on the basis of Freudian psychology as understood by amateurs twenty-five years ago. It arose, said he, out of a guilt complex of Southern men who had illicit relations with Negro women. But the cult of woman flourished in Europe, where there were few Negroes, in the days of medieval chivalry. Indeed, one of the sources of this cult in the South was the ideal of the medieval knight presented in Scott's novels and books such as *Scottish Chiefs* that impressionable Southern youths read. More important was the strength of the family in the South of the nineteenth century, in which the wife and mother played the supreme role, as well as the Southern cult of masculine virility, in which the sexes, in contrast with conditions today, were clearly differentiated.

Far deeper and more inhibiting to progress than this transitory sentiment were the racial attitudes inherited from the old order, which were reinforced and accentuated by events and forces that occurred years after the Confederate flags were furled. There had existed in the American colonies a folk prejudice against the Negro, but the pro-slavery propaganda had given it a religious basis and had indoctrinated the Southern people with the belief that the Negro was innately and permanently inferior to the white man (an idea widely held also in the North). The most important confrontation in the post-war South with this deeply rooted prejudice occurred, not in the power struggle in politics, but in the opposition to Negro education and civil rights. The Methodist Negro Bishop Lucius Holsey is quoted by Mann in his life of Atticus Haygood as saying as late as the turn of the nineteenth century: "The great majority of Southern white people hold that education ruins the Negro."

Against this powerful prejudice, Gustavus J. Orr, Superintendent of Public Schools for the state of Georgia from 1872 to 1887, Atticus G. Haygood, president of the struggling

Methodist college of Emory in Georgia, and Jabez L. M. Curry, agent of the George Peabody fund for education in the Southern states, fought valiantly and effectively. In 1880 Haygood delivered a forward-looking address entitled "The New South" in which he condemned certain of the Old South attitudes, and urged speedy reconciliation with the North and the development of an enlightened philosophy of progress. During the following year he published a little book entitled *Our Brother in Black, His Freedom and His Future*. In this book he discarded the prevailing view of permanent Negro inferiority by maintaining that some of the unfavorable characteristics shown by the Negro—his thoughtlessness and improvidence in regard to the future, his propensity to steal, to drink immoderately, and to "debase Christian worship"—were not inherited and permanent, but would pass away as he became better educated. He urged Southern whites to treat the Negroes as brothers, to educate them, and to encourage them to become property holders and to vote for literate candidates for public office.

In November, 1882, he was appointed General Agent of the Slater Fund for Negro education in the South, which had been created by an endowment of a Northern philanthropist. His first task in working for Negro education was to enlist the support of the churches of the common man in the South. To ex-President Rutherford B. Hayes, dominant member of the Slater board of Trustees, he wrote: "The Baptists & the Methodist absolutely control this country—the South I mean." He found that the senior Methodist bishops were hostile to Negro education. In an address before a Methodist gathering at Monteagle, Tennessee, on August 2, 1883, he discussed the controversial subject of the capacity of the Negro as compared with the whites to absorb education, an address that was later published in his volume *Pleas for Progress*. He declared that no one knew the intellectual capacity of the Negro, but that taking into account what small chance he had had and the short time in which he had been allowed to learn, he considered his achievements to be most remarkable. It would take several generations, he observed, to discover what the Negro's intellectual ability was, but he pointed out that already many individual Negroes had demonstrated their capacity for advanced education. He maintained, as did George Washington Cable two years later in his "The Freedman's Case in Equity," that there was no valid basis for fear that the education of the Negro would bring about social equality and he strongly condemned those prejudiced Southerners who looked down upon a white man or woman simply because he or she taught Negroes. Haygood worked mightily to increase not only the self-respect of the Negro himself but the respect of Southern whites for Negroes.

Nevertheless, he shared some of the denigrating prejudices of his time and region. He favored separate schools for whites and blacks, primarily, "because the South would accept no other; right or wrong; wise or foolish, this is a fact." He understood the fear of Southerners of race amalgamation. Even such a bold liberal as George Washington Cable, who aroused the wrath of the Southern people by advocating the granting of equal political and civil rights to the Negroes, did not go so far as to advocate mixed schools. Moreover, Haygood, like Curry and Booker T. Washington, believed that the primary task in educating the Negro was industrial education, to teach him a skilled trade. Haygood did not protest against segregation nor against the low wages they received, nor, until 1886, did he publicly attack the convict lease system that was so highly discriminatory against the Negro. Deeply religious, he held fast to the old faith and resisted the incursion of modern science and rationalism into this heritage from the past. Indeed, he must be considered as an outstanding transitional figure between the passing of the Old and the rise of the New South.

In the twenty years between the date of the South's secession from the Union and the beginning of the "New South" propaganda, the change toward a new order of society had been exceedingly slow. Not until approximately 1880 did the former Confederate states recover in the production of their staple crops to the pre-war yields — in sugar, not until 1889. Nor had the Southern people as a whole (the city folk to some degree excepted) changed greatly in their manners, customs, religion, and philosophy from those of the soldiers in gray who fought to establish a Southern republic. It could be said of the South of 1880, and even of 1890, what the Dutch scholar, Johan Huizinga observed of France and the Netherlands of the fourteenth and fifteenth centuries in his superb study, *The Waning of the Middle Ages,* that "the diapason of life had not changed." Just as those countries remained medieval at heart, so did the South in 1880 remain strongly attached to the values and philosophy of the Old South, with the one important exception that relatively few regretted the passing of slavery. Despite the trauma of defeat and the political upheaval of Reconstruction, much of the Old South survived, waning very gradually. The old continued to co-exist with the new until the twentieth century, somewhat like the relationship of an older brother with a younger one — at times in reverence, at other times in conflict, but ultimately in compromise. With the waning of the Old South civilization there passed away from the American scene much that was admirable (along with its evils) and much that would have given a needed variety to the texture of American life.

A Note on the Sources

(principally the primary sources)

CHAPTER I

THE PRINCIPAL MANUSCRIPT SOURCES OF THIS CHAPTER ARE: THE Alexander H. Stephens Papers, 115 volumes; the Andrew Johnson Papers, Vol. I (1839-59) ; the extensive Moses Waddell Diary, in the Library of Congress; the diary of Ferdinand Steel, a small farmer of Mississippi, owned by Professor Edward M. Steel, Jr., of West Virginia University; T. J. Knight, "Account of Newton Knight," also a Mississippi yeoman, the father of the author, in the Louisiana State Department of Archives and History; Micajah Clark's Travel Journal from Mississippi to South Carolina, in South Caroliniana Library, Columbia; Francis Orray Ticknor Papers, Duke University Library; the letters of William Harris Garland (a mechanic) and the diary and papers of David L. Swain, who arose from the lowly yeoman class to become governor of North Carolina and president of the state university, in the Southern Collection of the University of North Carolina (hereafter cited as the Southern Collection only) ; the Lulbegrud Baptist Church and the Providence Baptist Church minutes, the Augustus Woodward diary, the William Moody Pratt (Lexington, Kentucky, preacher) Diary, 1838-1891, 5 vols.; the Dicken-Troutman-Balke Papers; and a student's notebook taken on the lectures of Alexander Campbell in a course in religion at Bethany College, Virginia, in 1850, in the University of Kentucky Library.

Certain travelers in the ante-bellum South were interested in the common people and made observations about them and their mode of life. A selective list includes: William Thomson (a wool-carder and spinner), *Travels in the United States and Canada in the Years 1840, 41, and 42* (Edinburgh, 1842); Charles Lanman, *Letters from the Alleghany Mountains* (New York, 1849); Henry Benjamin Whipple, *Bishop Whipple's Southern Diary, 1843-1844,* ed. by L. B. Shippee (Minneapolis, 1937); James Silk Bucking-ham, *The Slave States of America* (London, 1842), 2 vols.; G. W. Featherstonhaugh, *Excursion Through the Slave States* (London, 1844), 2 vols.; Fredrika Bremer, *The Homes of the New World: Impressions of America* (New York, 1853), 2 vols.; Solon Rob-inson's letters in *Solon Robinson, Pioneer and Agriculturist,* ed. by Herbert A. Kellar (Indianapolis, 1936), 2 vols.; James Sterling, *Letters from the Slave States* (London, 1857); Frederick Law Olmsted, *A Journey in the Seaboard Slave States* (New York, 1856), *A Journey in the Back Country* (New York, 1860), and *A Journey through Texas* (New York, 1860); Ernst von Hesse-Wartegg, *Nord Amerika*—especially "Mississippi Fahrten"—(Leipzig, 1879), and Sir George Campbell, *White and Black: the Outcome of a Visit to the United States* (New York, 1879). Thomas D. Clark, ed., *Travels in the Old South; A Bibliography* (Norman, 1956-59), 4 vols., gives a critical description.

Other primary sources are: Daniel R. Hundley, *Social Rela-tions in Our Southern States* (New York, 1860); there is a short manuscript diary of Hundley in the Southern Collection, and Blanche H. C. Weaver has published a perceptive article entitled "D. R. Hundley, Pioneer Sociologist" in *The Georgia Review,* X (Summer, 1956), 222-234; Rebecca Latimer Felton, *Country Life in the Days of My Youth* (Athens, 1919); "Martin Mar-shall's Book," edited by Weymouth T. Jordan under the title, *Herbs, Hoecakes, and Husbandry* (Tallahassee, 1960); Kemp Battle, *Memories of an Old-Time Tarheel,* ed. by W. J. Battle (Chapel Hill, 1945). The writings of the Southern humorists often give authentic pictures of yeomen and cracker types and descriptions of their mores. I have cited an extensive list of their works in the bibliography of the chapter entitled "The Southern Yeoman: the Humorists' View and the Reality," in *The Mind of the Old South* (Baton Rouge, 1967), chap. VII, and pp. 319-320. The titles of the various collections of short stories and sketches of the country people of ante-bellum and post-bellum Georgia by Colonel Richard Malcolm Johnston are listed in the text; his autobiography, entitled *Autobiography of Col. Richard Malcolm Johnston* (Washington, 1901), is also a valuable source of the time.

Of secondary sources, I especially recommend: Frank L. Owsley, *Plain Folk of the Old South* (Baton Rouge, 1949); Blanche Henry Clark, *The Tennessee Yeomen, 1840-1860* (Nashville, 1942); Roger Shugg, *Origins of the Class Struggle in Louisiana: A Social History of White Farmers and Laborers During Slavery and After, 1840-1875* (Baton Rouge, 1939); Herbert Weaver, *Mississippi Farmers, 1850-1860* (Nashville, 1945); James C. Bonner, "Plantation and Farm, the Agricultural South," in Arthur S. Link and Rembert W. Patrick, eds., *Writing Southern History* (Baton Rouge, 1965), hereafter cited as Link and Patrick, *Writing Southern History;* Bell I. Wiley, *The Plain People of the Confederacy* (Baton Rouge, 1944), and William K. Scarborough, *The Overseer: Plantation Management in the Old South* (Baton Rouge, 1966). I have discussed the role of the common people in the Old South in a chapter entitled, "Discovery of the Middle Class," in *The Growth of Southern Civilization, 1790-1860* (New York, 1961), chap. 7.

CHAPTER II

The papers and plantation journals of the planters that have been preserved are quite extensive. Among the largest and most valuable are: James H. Hammond Papers and Diary in the Library of Congress and the South Caroliniana Library; the John Berkeley Grimball (a South Carolina rice planter) Papers, Ebenezer Pettigrew Papers, Private Diary of Edmund Ruffin (part in the Library of Congress), the Magnolia Plantation Journal, 1852-1862, and the Maunsel White Papers in the Southern Collection; the James Monette Plantation Diary, the William C. Rives Papers, and Joel R. Poinsett Papers in the Library of Congress; Henry Watson Papers in Duke University Library; the John McDonogh Papers and Samuel Walker, "Diary of a Louisiana Planter" in Tulane University Library; the William J. Minor and Alexander F. Pugh Collections at Louisiana State Department of Archives; Thomas B. Chaplin Plantation Journal, South Carolina Historical Society; Bedford Family Papers and the Buckner Family Papers, University of Kentucky Library; the John Hartwell Cocke Papers, and the Richard Eppes Plantation Journal in the Alderman Library, University of Virginia; the John Witherspoon DuBose Papers, especially "Autobiographical" and "The Canebrake Negro in 1850-1860," in Alabama State Department of Archives.

Published diaries and papers of the planters include: Edwin A. Davis, ed., *Plantation Life in the Florida Parishes of Louisiana 1836-1844, as Reflected in the Diary of Bennet H. Barrow* (New York, 1943); J. C. Bonner, ed., "Plantation Experiences of a New York Woman," *North Carolina Historical Review,* XXXIII (1956), 384-417 and 529-546; Charles L. Wagandt, ed., "The Civil War Journal of Dr. Samuel A. Harrison," *Civil War History,* XIII (June, 1967), 131-146; Betsy Fleet and Clement Eaton, eds., *Green Mount: A Virginia Plantation Family During the Civil War* (Lexington, 1962); J. S. Bassett, *The Westover Journal of John A. Selden* (Northampton, Mass., 1921); J. H. Easterby, ed., *The South Carolina Rice Plantation, as Revealed in the Papers of Robert F. W. Allston* (Chicago, 1945); J. C. Sitterson, ed., "Magnolia Plantation, 1852-1862: A Decade of a Louisiana Sugar Estate," *Mississippi Valley Historical Review,* XXV (Sept., 1938), 197-210; W. B. Hesseltine, ed., *Dr. J. G. M. Ramsey: Autobiography and Letters* (Nashville, 1954); Katherine Jones, ed., *The Plantation South* (Indianapolis, 1957); Ina Van Noppen, ed., *The South: A Documentary History* (Princeton, 1957); and Spencer B. King, Jr., *Georgia Voices: A Documentary History to 1872* (Athens, 1966). Clement Eaton, ed., *The Leaven of Democracy; the Growth of the Democratic Spirit in the Time of Jackson* (New York, 1963), gives a comparative view of Southern society with Northern society.

In addition to the travel accounts previously cited, the travelers who drew rather favorable pictures of the planters are: Sir Charles Lyell, *A Second Visit to the United States of North America* (London, 1848); Captain Basil Hall, *Travels in North America in the Years 1827-1828* (Edinburgh, 1830); Tyrone Power, *Impressions of America During the Years 1833, 1834, and 1835* (Philadelphia, 1836); Francis J. Grund, *Aristocracy in America* (New York, 1959); A. Dupuy Van Buren, *Jottings of a Year's Sojourn in the South* (Battle Creek, Mich., 1859); William H. Russell, *My Diary North and South* (Boston, 1863) and Catherine C. Hopley, *Life in the South from the Commencement of the War,* with and introduction by Clement Eaton (New York, 1968).

Other primary sources relating to the planters are: as to their libraries, a manuscript "Liste de mes livres, faite en Marz 1829" by Charles Gayarré, in the Gayarré Papers, Louisiana Department of Archives; a typescript of the books in the Bremo Plantation, Virginia, library made by P. St. Julian Wilson in 1928, in the Alderman Library of the University of Virginia; as to religion, Bishop Jackson Kemper, "Diary of a Trip Down the Mississippi," MS in Tulane University Library; the William Moody Pratt diary, and the students' notebook on Alexander Campbell classroom lectures at Bethany College, previously listed in the University of Kentucky Library; and the John B. Minor Papers in the Alderman Library of the University of Virginia.

The secondary works on the planters and plantation life are so numerous that I can only list those referred to in the text and a few outstanding works: U. B. Phillips, *Life and Labor in the Old South* (Boston, 1929); Joseph K. Menn, *The Large Slaveholders of Louisiana—1860* (New Orleans, 1964); Lewis C. Gray, *History of Agriculture in the Southern United States to 1860* (Washington, 1933), 2 vols.; Fletcher Green, *Constitutional Development in the South Atlantic States, 1770-1860* (Chapel Hill, 1930), and "Democracy in the Old South," *Journal of Southern History,* XII (Feb., 1946), 1-18; Charles S. Sydnor, *The Development of Southern Sectionalism, 1819-1848* (Baton Rouge, 1948); Gustavus V. Dyer, *Democracy in the South Before the Civil War* (Nashville, 1906); Daniel M. Robison "From Tillman to Long; Some Striking Leaders of the Rural South," *Journal of Southern History,* III (Aug., 1937), 289-310; Walter Posey has published valuable studies of the religious sects in the South, especially "The Protestant Episcopal Church; an American Adaptation," *Journal of Southern History,* XXV (Feb., 1959), 3-30, and his most recent work, *Frontier Mission: A History of Religion West of the Southern Appalachians to 1860* (Lexington, 1966); U. B. Phillips, *American Negro Slavery,* ed. by Eugene Genovese (Baton Rouge, 1966) and Kenneth Stampp, *The Peculiar Institution, Slavery in the Ante-Bellum South* (New York, 1956); John Hope Franklin, *The Militant South, 1800-1861* (Cambridge, 1956); Charles B. Sellers, ed., *The Southerner as American* (Chapel Hill, 1960); William R. Taylor, *Cavalier and Yankee; the Old South and American National Character* (New York, 1961); Eaton, *The Mind of the Old South* (Enlarged edition, Baton Rouge, 1967); and J. C. Bonner, "Profile of a Late Ante-Bellum Community," *American Historical Review,* XLIX (July, 1944), 663-680.

Rembert W. Patrick, *Aristocrats in Uniform: Duncan L. Clinch* (Gainesville, Fla., 1963).

CHAPTER III

The principal manuscript sources for this chapter are the collection of Gayarré Papers in the Howard-Tilton Library of Tulane University and the larger collection of his papers in the Department of Archives and History of Louisiana State University. I owe a debt of gratitude to Virgil Bedsole, director of the latter, and to Mrs. Connie G. Griffiths of the Manuscript Division of the Tulane University Library for their kind assistance to me in my research. Other manuscript collections that contain material relating to Gayarré are: the George Washington Cable Papers, and a small collection of letters of William Gilmore Simms to Gayarré at Tulane University; the Grace King Papers in the Southern Collection; the Paul Hamilton Hayne Papers and the J. D. B. DeBow Papers at Duke University. In the Gayarré Papers at Tulane is the typescript of an autobiography written by Gayarré for Paul Hamilton Hayne in 1885, entitled "Biographical Sketch of Charles Gayarré; author of the History of Louisiana, Philip II, Fernando de Lemos, Aubert Dubayet, etc., etc.," 18 pages. In the Louisiana State University Department of Archives there is an unpublished manuscript entitled "The Quadroons of Louisiana"; also a small collection of Gayarré correspondence of 1888 is in the archives of Xavier University in New Orleans. Two Ph.D. dissertations (unpublished) have been written on the life of Gayarré, Earl N. Saucier, "Charles Gayarré, the Creole Historian," George Peabody College for Teachers, 1935, and Edward Socola, "Charles Gayarré, a Biography," University of Pennsylvania, 1954.

Published primary sources on Gayarré are to be found in: Paul Hamilton Hayne, "Charles Gayarré, the Statesman," and "Charles Gayarré, the Author," *The Southern Bivouac,* II (June, 1886), 28-37, and (August), 172-176; Grace King, "Biographical Sketch of Charles Gayarré," in Gayarré, *History of Louisiana* (New Orleans, 1903), Vol. I; E. A. Parsons, ed., "Some Inedited Gayarré Manuscripts," *Louisiana Historical Quarterly,* XXXII (April, 1950), 189-222; Joseph Bonome, ed., "Some Letters of Charles Gayarré on Literature and Politics, 1854-1885," [containing copies of letters in the Everts Duyckinck and George Bancroft Papers in the New York Public Library], *Ibid.,* 222-254; Mary C. Simms

Oliphant *et al*, eds., *The Letters of William Gilmore Simms* (Columbia, S. C., 1953-54). For contemporary reviews of Gayarré's works, see *Southern Quarterly Review,* IX (April, 1846); *De-Bow's Review,* I (May, 1846), 383-434, II, (April, 1847), 279-293, and XI (July, 1857), 1-7; *North American Review,* LXV (July, 1847), 1-30, and LXXX (April, 1885), 480-511.

For comparison of Gayarré as a historian with other American historians, see J. S. Bassett, *The Middle Group of American Historians* (New York, 1917); also Michael Kraus, *A History of American History* (New York, 1937); Harvey Wish, *The American Historian* (New York, 1960); Mason Wade, *Francis Parkman, Heroic Historian* (New York, 1942); M. A. De Wolf Howe, *The Life and Letters of George Bancroft* (New York, 1908); and Russell B. Nye, *George Bancroft; Brahmin Rebel* (New York, 1945). Bancroft wrote to Gayarré an undated letter (probably in the summer of 1854 shortly before the publication of Gayarré's third volume of his history of Louisiana) in which he said, "you are my guide, and you will know I respect your authority. You not only construct interesting and attractive narrative, but actually so far exhaust the subject that little is to be gleaned after you." (MS in the Louisiana State Department of Archives and History.) Next to Gayarré, the best Southern historians of the period were Albert James Pickett, *History of Alabama, and Incidentally of Georgia and Mississippi* (Birmingham, Ala., 1851, 1896) and Hugh Grigsby, a judicious Virginia scholar, who wrote able studies of the Virginia conventions of 1776 and 1788. For some modern criticisms of Gayarré, see Philip D. Uzee, "An Analysis of the Histories of Charles E. A. Gayarré," *Proceedings of La. Acad. of Sciences,* VII (1943), 120-128; Herbert H. Lang, "Charles Gayarré and the Philosophy of Progress," *Louisiana History,* III (Summer, 1962), 251-261, and his Ph.D. dissertation on "Nineteenth Century Historians from the Gulf Coast States," at the University of Texas; Wilfred B. Yearns, Jr., "Charles Gayarré, Louisiana's Literary Historian," *Louisiana Historical Quarterly,* XXXIII (April, 1950), 254-268; and, as an antidote for Gayarré's rather romantic view of the Creoles [shared by Grace King in her *Creole Families of New Orleans* (New York, 1921)] see Joseph Tregle, Jr., "Early New Orleans Society: A Reappraisal," *Journal of Southern History,* XVIII (Feb., 1952), 20-36; Jay B. Hubbell, *The South in American Literature, 1607-1900* (Durham, 1954), 650-657.

CHAPTER IV

As to manuscript sources, this chapter is based on the following: Journal of Gertrude Thomas of Georgia, Paul Hamilton Hayne Papers, J. B. D. De Bow Papers, Francis Orray Ticknor Papers, Clara Dargan McLean Papers, in Duke University Library; Daniel R. Hundley Diary, Laura Comer Diary, George Anderson Mercer Diary, Minutes of the Chatham Academy of Savannah, Georgia, Minutes of the University of North Carolina Trustees, and Grace King Papers, in the Southern Collection; Calvin H. Wiley Papers, William A. Graham Papers, and Catherine Edmondston Diary in the North Carolina Department of Archives and History; Mitchell King Diary, Charleston Library Society, South Carolina, Jabez L. M. Curry Papers, Library of Congress.

Numerous published diaries, reminiscences, and collections of letters reveal social and cultural conditions in the Confederacy, among which are: J. B. Jones, *A Rebel War Clerk's Diary at the Confederate States Capital,* ed. by Howard Swiggett (New York, 1935), 2 vols.; [Catherine C. Hopley], *Life in the South from the Commencement of the War by a Blockaded British Subject* (London, 1863), 2 vols.; Mary Boykin Chesnut, *A Diary from Dixie,* ed. by Ben Ames Williams (Boston, 1961); Mrs. Roger Pryor, *Reminiscences of Peace and War* (New York, 1924); Fleet and Eaton, *Green Mount;* Kate Stone, *Brockenburn: the Journal of Kate Stone, 1861-1868,* ed. by J. Q. Anderson (Baton Rouge, 1955); Constance Cary (Mrs. Burton Harrison), *Recollections, Grave and Gay* (New York, 1912); Eliza Andrews, *The War-Time Journal of a Georgia Girl, 1864-1865,* ed. by Spencer B. King, Jr., (Macon, 1960); Judith B. McGuire, *Diary of a Southern Refugee* (New York, 1867); Edward Younger, ed., *Inside the Confederate Government; the Diary of Robert Garlick Hill Kean* (New York, 1957); Phoebe Pember Yates, *A Woman's Story* (Jackson, Tenn., 1959); Oliphant, *Letters of William Gilmore Simms; The Journal of Julia LeGrand, New Orleans, 1862-1863* (Richmond, 1911); J. B. Hubbell, ed., "The War Diary of John Esten Cooke," *Journal of Southern History,* XIX (Nov., 1953); E. S. Miers, ed., *When the World Ended; the Diary of Emma LeConte* (New York, 1957).

Travel accounts afford some glimpses of the cultural life of the Confederacy as well as several diaries of invading Northern soldiers, notably Russell, *My Diary, North and South;* Fitzgerald Ross, *Cities and Camps of the Confederate States,* ed. by Richard

B. Harwell (Urbana, 1958); James A. L. Fremantle, *The Fremantle Diary—Three Months in the Southern States,* ed. by Walter Lord (Boston, 1954); Clement Eaton, ed., "Diary of an Officer in Sherman's Army Marching Through the Carolinas," *Journal of Southern History,* IX (Aug., 1943), 238-254; Oscar D. Winther, ed., *With Sherman to the Sea: the Civil War Letters, Diaries & Reminiscences of Theodore F. Upson* (Baton Rouge, 1943); see E. M. Coulter, ed., *Travels in the Confederate States: A Bibliography* (Norman, 1948, 1961).

Other primary materials on cultural life in the Confederacy are: A. D. Kirwan, ed., *The Confederacy* (New York, 1959); Thomas Cooper DeLeon, *Four Years in Rebel Capitals* (Mobile, 1890), and *Belles, Beaux, and Brains of the 60's* (New York, 1907); Katherine Jones, ed., *Heroines of Dixie; Confederate Women Tell Their Side of the War* (Indianapolis, 1958); J. K. Bettersworth and James W. Silver, eds., *Mississippi in the Confederacy* (Baton Rouge, 1961), 2 vols.; Charles H. Smith, *Bill Arp, So Called, A Side Show of the Southern Side of the War* (New York, 1866); James Davidson, *The Living Writers of the South* (New York, 1869); William Gilmore Simms, *War Poetry of the South* (New York, 1866); B. B. Minor, *The Southern Literary Messenger, 1834-1864* (New York, 1905); Marjorie L. Crandall, ed., *Confederate Imprints, a Check List Based Principally on the Collection of the Boston Athenaeum* (Boston, 1955).

Magazines and newspapers that were used in this study include: *The Southern Illustrated News, Southern Literary Messenger,* and *Southern Punch* of Richmond; *DeBow's Review; The Countryman* (Georgia); *The Index* (London); *Charleston Mercury; Charleston Courier;* the Richmond newspapers, *Enquirer,* the *Whig,* the *Examiner,* and the *Dispatch;* the *Chattanooga Rebel,* the *Southern Confederacy* (Atlanta), and the Nashville *Republican Banner.* See Harrison A. Trexler, "The Davis Administration and the Richmond Press, 1861-1865," *Journal of Southern History,* XVI (May, 1950), 177-195; and Franc Paul, "The Chattanooga Rebel," and R. A. Halley, "Narrative of the War History of the Memphis Appeal," in Tenn. Hist. Comm., *Tennessee, Old and New* (Nashville, 1946); and R. L. Brantley, *Georgia Journalism of the Civil War Period* (Nashville, 1929).

Much has been written on the military and political history of the Confederacy but relatively little on the cultural conditions. Mary Elizabeth Massey has made an excellent critical survey entitled "The Confederate States of America: the Home Front," in Link and Patrick, *Writing Southern History*. Richard B. Harwell has made important studies of culture in the Confederacy, including *Confederate Belles-Lettres; a Bibliography and Finding List* (Hattiesburg, Miss., 1941), *Confederate Music* (Chapel Hill, 1950), *Songs of the Confederacy* (New York, 1951), and "The Richmond Stage," *Civil War History*, I (1955), 295-304. Other works dealing with various aspects of Confederate society include: Lawrence F. London, "Confederate Literature and Its Publishers," in *Studies in Southern History in Memory of Albert Ray Newsome* (Chapel Hill, 1957); Bell I. Wiley, *The Life of Johnny Reb, the Common Soldier of the Confederacy* (Indianapolis, 1943); Francis B. Simkins and James W. Patton, *The Women of the Confederacy* (Richmond, 1936); A. L. Bill, *The Beleaguered City; Richmond, 1861-1865* (New York, 1946); Kenneth Coleman, *Confederate Athens* (Athens, 1968); F. F. Corley, *Confederate City, Augusta, Georgia, 1860-1865* (Columbia, 1960); P. F. Walker, *Vicksburg: a People at War, 1860-1865* (Chapel Hill, 1960); Gerald Capers, *Occupied City: New Orleans Under the Federals* (Lexington, 1965); John DeBerry, "Confederate Tennessee," Ph.D. dissertation, University of Kentucky, 1967; John K. Bettersworth, *Confederate Mississippi; the People and Policies of a Cotton State in War-Time* (Baton Rouge, 1943); T. Conn Bryan, *Confederate Georgia* (Athens, 1953); E. M. Coulter, *College Life in the Old South* (Athens, 1951); C. W. Dabney, *Universal Education in the South* (Chapel Hill, 1936); Ottis C. Skipper, *J. D. B. DeBow, Magazinist of the Old South* (Athens, 1958); Jay Hubbell, *South in American Literature;* W. Stanley Hoole, "Charleston Theatricals during the Tragic Decade, 1860-1869," *Journal of Southern History*, XI (Nov., 1945), 538; Edmund Wilson, *Patriotic Gore: Studies in the Literature of the American Civil War* (New York, 1962). For general histories that deal with culture as well as military and political affairs, see E. M. Coulter, *The Confederate States of America, 1861-1865* (Baton Rouge, 1950), and Clement Eaton, *A History of the Southern Confederacy* (New York, 1954).

CHAPTER V

The mood of a people is perhaps best revealed by intimate diaries, letters, and private papers not intended for publication.

Some of this type of source material which the author has used in this chapter are: Laura Comer Diary; Edward Clifford Anderson Diary; George Anderson Mercer Diary, 1855-85; in the Southern Collection of the University of North Carolina; Ella Gertrude Thomas Journal, in Duke University Library; the Dicken-Troutman-Balke Papers, in the University of Kentucky Library; and the John B. Minor Papers in the Alderman Library of the University of Virginia.

Printed sources include: Elizabeth McPherson, ed., "Letters from North Carolina to President Johnson," *North Carolina Historical Review*, XXVII (1950), 336-363; Cornelia Hancock, *South After Gettysburg, Letters of Cornelia Hancock, 1866-1868*, ed. by H. S. Jaquette (New York, 1956); Chesnut, *A Diary from Dixie;* Eliza Andrews, *The War-Time Journal of a Georgia Girl;* David C. Barrow, "A Georgia Plantation," *Scribner's Monthly*, XXI (April, 1881); Myrta L. Avary, *Dixie After the War* (New York, 1906); Henry Watterson, *Marse Henry, An Autobiography* (New York, 1919), 2 vols.; Susan Dabney Smedes, *Memorials of a Southern Planter*, ed. by Fletcher Green (New York, 1965); Albion W. Tourgee, *A Fool's Errand, by One of the Fools* (New York, 1879); Kemp Battle, *Memories of an Old-Time Tar Heel;* Mrs. Roger A. Pryor, *Reminiscences of Peace and War.*

One of the important sources for studying the mood of the South during the decade after the war, especially from 1865 to 1868, are the travels accounts. Most of the Northern travelers were Republicans, but they seemed to have tried to give an objective account. The earliest of these travelers were Whitelaw Reid, *After the War:A Tour of the Southern States, 1865-1860,* ed. by C. Vann Woodward (New York, 1965). Sidney Andrews, *The South Since the War* (Boston, 1860); John R. Dennett, *The South As It Is, 1865-1866,* ed. by H. M. Christman (New York, 1965); J. T. Trowbridge, *A Picture of the Desolated States and the Work of Restoration* (Hartford, 1868); and De Forest, *A Union Officer in the Reconstruction.* A few years later valuable observations on the South were made by Robert Somers, *The Southern States Since the War, 1870-71,* ed. by Malcolm C. McMillan (University, Ala., 1965); Edward King, *The Southern States of North America, A Record of Journeys* (London, 1875); Sir George Campbell, *White and Black, the Outcome of a Visit to the United States* (London, 1879); Charles Nordhoff, *The Cotton States in the Spring and Summer of 1875* (New York,

1876); Anderson, ed., *The Works of Sidney Lanier* (Baltimore, 1945).

Pertinent secondary works that contribute to understanding the Southern mood after Appomattox are: Phillips Russell, *The Woman Who Rang the Bell, the Story of Cornelia Phillips Spencer* (Chapel Hill, 1949); Joel Williamson, *After Slavery, the Negro in South Carolina During Reconstruction, 1861-1871* (Chapel Hill, 1965); J. T. Dorris, *Pardon and Amnesty Under Lincoln and Johnson; The Restoration of the Confederates to Their Rights and Privileges, 1861-1898* (Chapel Hill, 1955); Otto H. Olsen, *Carpetbagger's Crusade: The Life of Albion Winegar Tourgee* (Baltimore, 1965); Aubrey L. Brooks, *Walter Clark, Fighting Judge* (Chapel Hill, 1944); Henry L. Swint, *The Northern Teacher in the South, 1862-1870* (Nashville, 1941); Jonathan Daniels, *Prince of Carpetbaggers* (Philadelphia, 1958); T. D. Clark and A. D. Kirwan, *The South Since Appomattox* (New York, 1967); W. M. Evans, *Ballots and Fence Rails: Reconstruction on the Lower Cape Fear* (Chapel Hill, 1966); and Stanley M. Elkins, *Slavery: A Problem in American Institutional and Intellectual Life* (Chicago, 1959).

CHAPTER VI

The primary sources for this chapter are: Grace King Papers, and Laura Comer Diary, Southern Collection, the Charles E. A. Gayarré Papers in the Louisiana Department of Archives and History and Tulane University Library; Gayarré Papers, Xavier University, New Orleans; Paul Hamilton Hayne Papers, Duke University Library; Jabez L. M. Curry Papers, Library of Congress; Edwin A. Alderman Papers, especially MS, "Institute Statistics," two manuscript notebooks that are really a journal of observation in North Carolina in 1889-1890; Cornelia Phillips Spencer Papers in Archives of the North Carolina Department of History and Archives; Henry Clay Warmoth Papers, Southern Collection at University of North Carolina. Published primary sources that were used are: *The Papers of Walter Clark*, ed. by A. E. Brooks and Hugh T. Lefler (Chapel Hill, 1948), Vol. I (1857-1901); *The Life and Letters of Walter Hines Page*, ed. by Burton J. Hendrick (New York, 1924), Vol. 1; Henry Grady, *The New South* (New York, 1890); Joel Chandler Harris, *Life of Henry W. Grady, Including His Speeches* (New York, 1890);

Edgar Gardner Murphy, *Problems of The Present South* (New York, 1906); Smedes, *Memorials of a Southern Planter;* Grace King, *Memories of a Southern Woman of Letters;* Charles Gayarré, "The Southern Question," *North American Review,* Vol. 25 (Nov.-Dec., 1873), 472-498; Sidney Lanier, *Retrospects and Prospects* (New York, 1899), Chap. IV, "The New South"; George W. Cable, *The Negro Question: A Selection of Writings on Civil Rights in the South,* ed. by Arlin Turner (New York, 1958), containing his article "The Freedmen's Case in Equity"; Josephus Daniels, *Tar Heel Editor* (Chapel Hill, 1939); Charles Gayarré, "A Louisiana Sugar Plantation of the Old Regime," *Harper's Monthly Magazine,* March 1887; Charles Gayarré, "The Creoles of History and the Creoles of Romance," *Christmas Dixie* (Atlanta, December, 1888); John S. Kennedy, "The Last Days of Charles Gayarré," *Louisiana Historical Quarterly,* XV (July, 1932), 359-375; Anderson, ed., *The Works of Sidney Lanier;* Louis D. Rubin, Jr., ed., *Teach the Freeman: The Correspondence of Rutherford B. Hayes and the Slater Fund for Negro Education, 1881-1887* (Baton Rouge, 1959), 2 vols.; and previously cited travel accounts by John T. Trowbridge, Edward King, Charles Nordhoff, Robert Somers, and George Campbell. Also Frances Butler Leigh, *Ten Years on a Georgia Plantation Since the War* [1883] (New York, 1968). Atticus G. Haygood, *Our Brother in Black: His Freedom and His Future* (Nashville, 1881), and *The New South . . .* (Oxford, Ga., 1880).

Valuable secondary works in the study of the waning of the Old South civilization are: C. Vann Woodward, *Origins of the New South, 1877-1913* (Baton Rouge, 1951); Paul Buck, *The Road to Reunion, 1865-1900* (Boston, 1938), Paul Gaston "The New South," and George B. Tindall, "Southern Negroes Since Reconstruction, Dissolving the Static Image," Link and Patrick, *Writing Southern History;* Dumas Malone, *Edwin A. Alderman, A Biography* (New York, 1940); Burton J. Hendrick, *The Training of an American; the Earlier Life and Letters of Walter H. Page, 1855-1913* (Boston, 1928); Edwin Mims, *Sidney Lanier* (Boston, 1905); E. W. Parks, *Sidney Lanier* (New York, 1964); Aubrey H. Starke, *Sidney Lanier, a Biographical and Critical Study* (Chapel Hill, 1933); Harold Mann, *Atticus Haygood: Methodist Bishop, Editor, and Educator* (Athens, 1965); Charles R. Anderson, "Charles Gayarré and Paul Hayne: The Last Literary Cavaliers," *American Studies in Honor of William K. Boyd*

(Durham, 1940) ; J. Carlyle Sitterson, *Sugar Country, the Cane Sugar Industry in the South, 1753-1950* (Lexington, 1953) ; William B. Hesseltine, *Confederate Leaders in the New South* (Baton Rouge, 1950) ; Arlin Turner, *George W. Cable, A Biography* (Durham, 1956) ; L. C. Bikle, *George W. Cable, His Life and Letters* (New York, 1928) ; Clement Eaton, "Edwin A. Alderman—Liberal of the New South," *North Carolina Historical Review,* XXIII (April 1946), 206-221; John S. Ezell, *The South Since 1865* (New York, 1963) ; Roger W. Shugg, "Survival of the Plantation System in Louisiana," *Journal of Southern History,* III (Aug., 1937), 311-325; Thomas B. Alexander, "Persistent Whiggery in the Confederate South, 1860-1877," *Journal of Southern History,* XXVII (August, 1961), 305-329; Virginus Dabney, *Liberalism in the South* (Chapel Hill, 1932) ; H. C. Nixon, *Possum Trot, Rural Community South* (November, 1941) ; Walter Prichard, "The Effects of the Civil War on the Louisiana Sugar Industry," *Journal of Southern History,* V (August, 1939), 315-332; Nelson M. Blake, *William Mahone of Virginia, Soldier and Political Insurgent* (Richmond, 1935) ; Francis B. Simkins, "Robert Lewis Dabney, Southern Conservative," *Georgia Review,* XVIII (Winter, 1964), 393-407; C. Vann Woodward, *Tom Watson, Agrarian Rebel* (New York, 1938) ; J. F. Wall, *Henry Watterson, Reconstructed Rebel* (New York, 1956) ; Stuart Noblin, *Leonidas LaFayette Polk* (Chapel Hill, 1949) ; Thomas D. Clark, *Pills, Petticoats and Plows: the Southern Country Store* (Indianapolis, 1944) and *The Southern Country Editor* (Indianapolis, 1948) ; W. J. Cash, *The Mind of the South* (New York, 1941) ; Edwin A. Alderman and Armistead C. Gordon, *L. M. Curry, A Biography* (New York, 1901) ; R. B. Nixon, *Henry W. Grady, Spokesman of the New South* (New York, 1943).

Index